Lecture Notes in Computer Science   8359

Commenced Publication in 1973
Founding and Former Series Editors:
Gerhard Goos, Juris Hartmanis, and Jan van Leeuwen

Akiyo Nadamoto   Adam Jatowt
Adam Wierzbicki   Jochen L. Leidner (Eds.)

Social Informatics

SocInfo 2013 International Workshops
QMC and HISTOINFORMATICS
Kyoto, Japan, November 25, 2013
Revised Selected Papers

 Springer

Volume Editors

Akiyo Nadamoto
Konan University, Department of Intelligence and Informatics
8-9-1 Okamoto, Higashinada-ku, Kobe 658-0072, Japan
E-mail: nadamoto@konan-u.ac.jp

Adam Jatowt
Kyoto University, Graduate School of Informatics
Yoshida-Honmachi, Sakyo-ku, Kyoto 606-8501, Japan
E-mail: adam@dl.kuis.kyoto-u.ac.jp

Adam Wierzbicki
Polish-Japanese Institute of Information Technology
Ul. Koszykowa 86, 02-008 Warsaw, Poland
E-mail: adamw@pjwstk.edu.pl

Jochen L. Leidner
Thomson Reuters Corporate Research and Development
The Vintners Place, 68 Upper Thames Street, London EC4V 3BJ, UK
E-mail: jochen.leidner@thomsonreuters.com

ISSN 0302-9743   e-ISSN 1611-3349
ISBN 978-3-642-55284-7   e-ISBN 978-3-642-55285-4
DOI 10.1007/978-3-642-55285-4
Springer Heidelberg New York Dordrecht London

Library of Congress Control Number: 2014937290

LNCS Sublibrary: SL 3 – Information Systems and Application, incl. Internet/Web
and HCI

Typesetting: Camera-ready by author, data conversion by Scientific Publishing Services, Chennai, India

Printed on acid-free paper

Springer is part of Springer Science+Business Media (www.springer.com)

Preface

The Fifth International Conference on Social Informatics (SocInfo 2013) is an interdisciplinary venue for researchers from Computer Science, Informatics, Social Sciences and Management Sciences dedicated to sharing ideas and opinions and to presenting original research work at the intersection of socially-centric platforms and social phenomena. The workshops of SocInfo 2013 were held in Kyoto, Japan, on November 25th, 2013. Among the proposals submitted in response to the call for workshops, we decided to convene the following two workshops:

- First Workshop on Quality, Motivation and Coordination of Open Collaboration (QMC 2013)
- First International Workshop on Histoinformatics (HISTOINFORMATICS 2013)

The research area of SocInfo is growing rapidly and the topics of each workshop cover specific areas of social informatics. The QMC 2013 workshop attracted research papers on new algorithms or methods that attempt to either improve the quality of open collaboration, to increase the motivation of open collaboration, to reduce the cost of financial motivation or to decrease the time needed to finish collaborative tasks, for example through better coordination. The Histoinformatics 2013 workshop gathered papers that aim at improving interaction between computer science and historical science towards fostering a new research direction of computational history. These proceedings contain all the papers accepted at the SocInfo 2013 workshops.

We would like to thank the authors of submitted papers and participants for making the workshops successful. We express our gratitude to the workshops' organizers and all reviewers for their hard work. We also thank Matthew Rowe, Antal van den Bosch and Roger Evans for delivering exciting keynote and invited talks. We hope that you will find this program interesting and thought-provoking.

February 2014

Akiyo Nadamoto
Adam Jatowt
Adam Wierzbicki
Jochen L. Leidner

Organization

Workshop Committee Co-Chairs

Akiyo Nadamoto   Konan University, Japan
Jochen L. Leidner   Thomson Reuters, United Kingdom

First Workshop on Quality, Motivation and Coordination of Open Collaboration (QMC 2013)

Workshop Chair

Adam Wierzbicki   Polish-Japanese Institute of Information
                        Technology, Poland

First International Workshop on Histoinformatics (HISTOINFORMATICS 2013)

Workshop Co-Chair

Adam Jatowt   Kyoto University, Japan
Gael Dias   Normandie University, France
Agostini-Ouafi Viviana Normandie University, France
Christian Gudehus   University of Flensburg, Germany
Gunter Muhlberger   University of Innsbruck, Austria

Platinum Sponsors

Bronze Sponsors

Other Sponsors

Supporters

Table of Contents

First Workshop
on Quality, Motivation
and Coordination of Open
Collaboration (QMC 2013)

Measurement Quality of Online Collaboration in Presence of Negative Relationships

Mikołaj Morzy, Tomasz Bartkowski, and Krzysztof Jędrzejewski

Institute of Computing Science
Poznan University of Technology
Piotrowo 2, 60-965 Poznan, Poland
Mikolaj.Morzy@put.poznan.pl

Abstract. Online collaboration services usually focus on positive relationships between constituting actors. Many environments in which social mechanisms are present harness positive feedback of social recognition, status visibility, or collective action. Simple mechanisms of commenting on status updates and up-voting of resources attributed to an actor may result in proverbial karma flow in the socially aware online collaboration environment. On the other hand, many services allow users to also express their dislike, irritation and contempt towards resources provided by users. For instance, down-voting mechanics is crucial in online news aggregation services, such as Digg or Reddit, to maintain a certain level of quality of presented contents. Despite the availability of data, not many works have been published on measuring the negative network effects in social networks. In this paper we analyze a large body of data harvested from a Polish online news aggregation site Wykop.pl and we examine the effects of a more considerate approach to negative network construction when measuring the overall parameters and characteristics of the social network derived from positive (up-voting) and negative (down-voting) behaviors of users.

1 Introduction

Most contemporary online collaboration services and social networks focus explicitly on positive relationships between actors. Users of Facebook have hundred possibilities to express their content towards people, products, places or services, but have little opportunity to file a complaint or express their dislike. Practically the only available mechanism of producing a negative relationship is by posting a negative and aggressive comment. However, in order to discover such comment one has to employ sentiment analysis techniques and opinion mining algorithms, which may be prohibitively time-consuming. Even satirical fan-pages of many services, people, and brands, aimed clearly as parodies, are linked via positive relationship with exactly the entities that these fan-pages criticize. Another option is un-friending an actor of a social network, but discovering the true semantics of such event may be more difficult depending on the context. The lack of negative relationships presented *expressis verbis* thus makes the analysis of negative networks even more challenging.

A. Nadamoto et al. (Eds.): SocInfo 2013 Workshops, LNCS 8359, pp. 3–13, 2014.

A naive approach to negative social network analysis is to treat every single instance of a negative event as a proxy for a negative relationship between agents. By negative event we mean every expressed behavior that may have negative semantics associated with it. One may collect all negative events reported in the data, and then use these events to add negative edges to the network. Indeed, many studies present in the literature take this simplistic approach. We argue that focusing on social network analysis, without proper understanding of the implicit meaning of negative relationships, leads to skewed results and paints a picture of a negative network which is partially not supported by evidence. To support our claim we have collected a large body of behavioral data from a Polish online news aggregation service and we have performed a comparative analysis of several types of negative social networks constructed using varying degrees of negative edge intensity. The preliminary results of our experiments suggest that a naive approach to negative network formation may indeed lead to skewed results of SNA metrics. In order to secure measurement quality one has to use a more nuanced approach when constructing negative networks.

Our paper is organized as follows. First, we describe previous work related to our research in Section 2. Section 3 describes the dataset used in the experiments. Then, we introduce basic models of negative and positive networks in Section 4. We present the results of conducted experiments in Section 5. Finally, we conclude the paper in Section 6 with a short summary.

2   Related Work

One of the first persons to study the dynamics of interpersonal relations, with a special impact on negative relationships, was Fritz Heider, who has created the balance theory to explain the attitude change over time [4]. The balance theory was subsequently extended by Harary and Cartwright, who introduced the notion of the structural balance [3]. Dyadic and triadic analysis became prevalent and P-O-X tuples model was commonly used to represent the instability of relationships. A more modern approach was born at the same time when first online social networks began to appear. Essembly, which is as of this writing closed, was a social network service aimed at exchange of political views and opinions. Data collected from the website allowed Brzozowski *et al.* to perform interesting analysis of online friendships and enmities [2]. The work contains a very detailed report on the quantitative analysis of the network, with some emphasis on negative relationships. The authors stress the importance of recommendation mechanisms in the network, and provide some evidence for the existence of homophily in the network. Our research is conducted on the dataset harvested from an online news aggregation service Wykop.pl. This website is a clone of popular news aggregating services, such as Digg, Reddit, and Slashdot. The latter was created in 1999 and in 2002 was expanded with Slashdot Zoo, a service allowing users to mark other users of the service explicitly as friends or foes. The data collected from Slashdot Zoo was analyzed by Kunegis *et al.* [5]. The authors find evidence for the balance theory, observe the multiplicative transitivity rule ("the enemy of my enemy is my friend"), and examine various network centrality measures, such as degree centrality or betweenness centrality. Explicit negative relationships and their effect on work organizations was researched by Labianca and Brass [6]. The main conclusion drawn by the authors is that negative relationships have a greater influence on work organization and productivity than positive relationships. The same authors examined also the effect of negative edges on resolving intergroup conflicts within a single organization [1]. Mining of social networks in search of predictive patterns has been the subject of numerous works. For instance, in [7] Leskovec *et al.* present algorithms for predicting the existence of both positive and negative links. The authors explore datasets from Epinions.com, Slashdot, and Wikipedia. We are influenced by this work in that we also use probabilistic models to estimate the probability of an edge existence. However, Leskovec *et al.* used the connection patterns between hidden nodes and their direct neighbors. whereas we are focusing only on the direct cooperation between users. Similar work has been performed in the domain of psychology where social networks were scrutinized in search of models of unethical behavior [1].

3   Dataset

To collect data we have decided to use the public API of Wykop.pl online news aggregation site. Wykop is a typical social news site, where registered users may submit links to interesting and valuable contents found on the Web, and the voting mechanism provides additional social filtering and ranking of discovered resources. Registered users may evaluate submitted resources by up-voting (which is tantamount to recommending a given resource) and down-voting (which gradually lowers the visibility of the resource). The life-cycle of a resource is the following: all resources submitted during the last 24 hours are placed in a staging area called *The Excavation* and have a limited time to escape from there. Users *kick out* (up-vote) links or bury (down-vote) links based on their evaluation of the quality of a link. Popular links may be promoted all the way to the home page, where they enjoy the infamous Slashdot effect (a short burst of huge traffic generated by the online news aggregation site). The service does not reveal the details of the algorithm that governs the life-cycle of resources to counteract possible attempts to game the system and gain unearned traffic.

Wykop offers an API for gathering data on users, resources, and actions. The API uses HTTP and REST protocols to provide data served in JSON and XML formats. The functionality of the API allows to browse the contents of the home page, reading the details of submitted resources (including user comments), adding, kicking out, and burying of resources, or using the microblogging service associated with the service. In our experiments we have gathered data on two types of objects. First, we have gathered data on submitted links, and for each link we have downloaded meta-data, the number of kick-outs and the number of buries. Next, we have collected data on users by browsing their profiles and reading information on the links they have submitted, kicked-out, or buried.

We have collected data on all links submitted to the service between December 28th 2005, and April 10th 2009. The dataset consists of 158 683 links that have been kicked-out 4 017 482 times, and have been buried 547 229 times. We have also gathered data on 25 596 users who submitted at least one link, 18 949 users who buried at least one link, and 49 667 users who kicked-out at least one link. The total number of user profiles downloaded from Wykop.pl is 59 217, and among them 51 814 expressed any emotion towards presented content by kicking out or burying at least one resource. We note a surprisingly high number of users who do not express any behavior (either positive or negative), and we notice that the number of buries far outnumbers the number of submissions, although the number of burying users is lower than the number of users who provide new contents.

4 Basic Definitions

The basic network model used in this research is the following. There are four distinct sets of items:

- $U = \{u_1, \ldots, u_m\}$ - a set of users,
- $I = \{i_1, \ldots, i_n\}$ - a set of items,
- $A^+ = \{a_1^+, \ldots, a_p^+\}$ - a set of up-vote actions (where $a_i^+ = (u_k, i_l)$ denotes the fact that the user u_k kicked out item i_l),
- $A^- = \{a_1^-, \ldots, a_r^-\}$ - a set of down-vote actions (where $a_i^- = (u_k, i_l)$ denotes the fact that the user u_k buried item i_l).

Our goal is to build two graphs, representing the positive and negative network, respectively. The positive network is represented by the graph $G^+ = (V, E^+)$, where the set of vertices $V \subseteq U$, and the set of edges E^+ consists of pairs of users between whom we can identify positive relationships. Analogously, the negative network is modeled as the graph $G^- = (V, E^-)$, where the set of vertices $V \subseteq U$, and the set of edges E^- consists of pairs of users connected via negative relationships. Of course, a naive approach would be to use sets A^+ and A^- instead of E^+ and E^-. Such networks would treat the existence of a positive/negative action as sufficient reason for building emotionally loaded relationship. We argue that this approach is not only naive and simplistic, but it leads to skewed network measurements and requires significant refinement.

4.1 Vertices

Before we proceed any further we have to examine in detail the set of users in search of outliers. Since we are interested in improving the quality and reliability of network statistics, we need to take into consideration possible existence of special vertices with outlier characteristics. We posit that there are two special cases of users present in online news aggregation service:

- *haters* : these are the users who tend to down-vote every resource displayed in the service, no matter what the quality of the resource is (as measured by the ratings of other users),

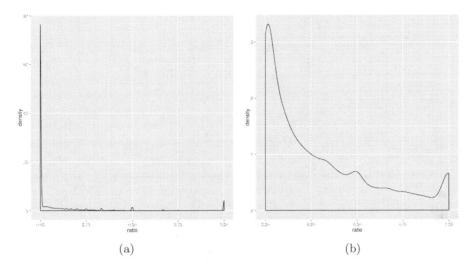

Fig. 1. Distribution of (a) haters and (b) spammers in the dataset

– *spammers* : these users provide consistently resources of dubious quality, hidden advertisement, offensive contents, etc.

Figure 1 presents the distributions of the ratios of buries to all actions (kick-outs and buries) for all users. As we can see, haters form a very distinctive group. Almost all users have the ratio close to 0 (meaning that these users far more frequently kick out interesting contents than bury uninteresting findings). Usually, users try to punish submissions that have been previously posted on the website (so called *reposts*). However, there is a small group of users (3.6%) who bury over 95% resources, and this small group can be seen in Figure 1(a) as a small spike close to the value of 1. For spammers the ratio is less distinctive, but we still see that the vast majority of users has the ratio of down-voted contents to all submitted contents way below 0. Again, in Figure 1(b) we see a very characteristic spike around the value 1. Of all users who submit contents 5.8% of users have the spam ratio of 0.95 or more. Therefore, we set the parameters $\alpha_{hate} = 0.95$ and $\alpha_{spam} = 0.95$ as threshold for identifying a user as a hater or spammer, respectively.

4.2   Edges

In order to create edges in the network we have decided to use two different approaches to deciding on the nature of relationship between any two users, represented as vertices in the network. Below we describe our edge creation models in detail.

Baseline Model. In the simplest model for each pair of users we compute the number of times users kicked out or buried their items. Depending on the result of the comparison of these two measurements we label the relationship as positive or negative. Let $I(u_j)$ denote the set of items submitted by the user u_j. For each pair of users we compute the value:

$$\beta(u_i, u_j) = \frac{|A^+(u_i, u_j)|}{|A^-(u_i, u_j)|}$$

where $A^+(u_i, u_j) = \{a_p^+ = (u_i, i_p) : i_p \in I(u_j)\}$ is the set of items i_p submitted by the user u_j and up-voted by the user u_i. Similarly, $A^-(u_i, u_j) = \{a_r^- = (u_i, i_r) : i_r \in I(u_j)\}$ is the set of items i_r submitted by the user u_j and down-voted by the user u_i. If $\beta(u_i, u_j) < 1$ then the user u_i more often down-votes the items of the user u_j and we attribute the negative orientation to their relationship, whereas when $\beta(u_i, u_j) > 1$ then the relationship between the users is positive. Please note that the relationship does not need to be reflexive, i.e. the user u_i can have positive feelings towards the user u_j and at the same time the user u_j may have a negative attitude towards u_i. If there are no explicit actions (up-votes and down-votes) between a given pair of users, an edge is not created between these users.

Probability Models. Probability models use the same main principle which is to create an edge between vertices if and only if the observed sentiment differs significantly from the expected sentiment. In other words, each model computes the *a priori* probability of positive and negative relationship between users. Then, we compare the estimates with the *a posteriori* behavior displayed in the collected data. If the observed behavior is sufficiently different, for instance, if the model predicts a positive relationship between users u_i and u_j, but the data reveal consistent down-voting of u_j's contents by the user u_i, we create an edge representing the relationship displayed in the data.

To present the first probability model we need to introduce the notation used throughout the remainder of the section. Let us denote the following probabilities (analogous probabilities are used for down-voting items):

- $p^+(u_i, u_j, i_n)$: the probability that the user u_i will up-vote the item i_n knowing that the item has been submitted by the user u_j,
- $p^+(u_i, *, *)$: the probability that the user u_i will up-vote any item, regardless of who submitted the item,
- $p^+(*, u_i, *)$: the probability that a random item submitted by the user u_i will be up-voted,
- $p^+(*, *, i_n)$: the probability that a random user will up-vote the item i_n,
- $p^+(u_i, *, i_n)$: the probability that the user u_i will up-vote the item i_n,
- $p^+(u_i, u_j, *)$: the probability that the user u_i will up-vote any item submitted by the user u_j.

The first probability model, referred to as Model A, assumes, that the probability of up-voting an item is independent of the user who has submitted the item. In other words, Model A assumes that users decide to up-vote or down-vote the item solely based on their evaluation of the item, and they do not consider the origin of the item. According to Model A, the probability of up-voting by the user u_i of a particular item i_n submitted by the user u_j can be approximated as ($\hat{p}$ denotes the expected probability):

$$\hat{p}^+(u_i, u_j, i_n) = p^+(u_i, *, i_n) \approx p^+(u_i, *, *) \cdot p^+(*, *, i_n)$$

The second probability model, called unimaginatively Model B, posits that users are aware of who submitted a link and may modify their behavior depending on the source of the submission. We assume that users are more forgiving towards users who regularly supply high quality material, but occasionally post uninteresting contents. In such case users may "forgive" and use the reputation of the submitting user as a proxy for the real evaluation of the quality of the item. Similarly, when an item is submitted by the user who consistently provides low quality contents, other users will tend to down-vote the item even if the item is of good quality (in other words, the item would not have been down-voted had it been submitted by someone else). Mathematically we express Model B as:

$$\hat{p}^+(u_i, u_j, i_n) = p^+(u_i, u_j, i_n) \approx p^+(u_i, *, *) \cdot \max\{p^+(*, *, i_n), p^+(*, u_j, *)\}$$

The final probability model, called Model C, discards the evaluation of the item altogether and assumes, that the probability of up-voting between users depends only on independent probabilities representing the tendency of a user to up-vote and the likelihood of having user's content up-voted. The model can be expressed as:

$$\hat{p}^+(u_i, u_j, *) \approx p^+(u_i, *, *) \cdot p^+(*, u_j, *)$$

In all the above models an edge is created in the graph between vertices representing users u_i and u_j if the observed probability of up-voting is significantly larger than the expected probability of up-voting. The parameter γ is called the *sensitivity* of the model and can be changed to construct networks of different shapes and properties.

- for Models A and B: $p^+(u_i, u_j, i_n) \geq \gamma \cdot \hat{p}^+(u_i, u_j, i_n)$
- for Model C: $p^+(u_i, u_j, *) \geq \gamma \cdot \hat{p}^+(u_i, u_j, *)$

Analogous computation is performed for negative edges and negative relationships, we skip the equations for the sake of brevity but we believe that the formulas for the negative relationship edges are self-evident.

The above models have been used to create several networks with positive and negative relationships. We have used these networks to compare the properties of networks and to compute the degree of bias introduced when positive and negative relationships are posited without due consideration. We have built the following types of networks:

- N_0: the original network with all vertices and edges created by the baseline model,
- N_1^A: the network with all vertices and edges created by Model A,
- N_1^B: the network with all vertices and edges created by Model B,
- N_1^C: the network with all vertices and edges created by Model C,
- N_2^C: the network with haters and spammers removed, only negative edges created by Model C.

5   Experiments

The N_0 network serves as the baseline comparison for our further models. This network has been built from the data on 51 814 users who up-voted or down-voted at least one item and 25 596 users who have submitted at least one item. The positive relationship network N_0^+ consists of 56 565 vertices and 2 927 050 edges, and the negative relationship network N_0^- consists of 29 403 vertices and 410 081 edges. For the probability models A, B, and C we needed to assume some value of the sensitivity parameter γ. Recall that in Model A the edge is created if the observed probability of up-voting $p^+(u_i, u_j, i_n)$ is greater than $\gamma \cdot \hat{p}^+(u_i, u_j, i_n)$. Thus, we have computed the number of edges which are created depending on the values of the sensitivity parameter γSince the observed probability of up-voting or down-voting an item always equals 1, we have to examine only the distribution of $\hat{p}^+(u_i, u_j, i_n)$. The results are depicted in Figure 2.

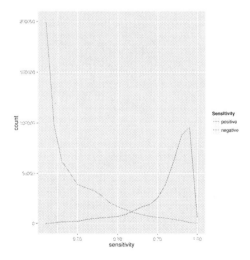

Fig. 2. The number of positive and negative edges w.r.t. the sensitivity parameter γ

We have divided the distribution into three terciles representing possible emotional states of negative discrimination (dislike), indifference, and positive discrimination (likeness). We have decided to ignore all situations in which the perceived behavior of a user fell into the third tercile. In other words, if the expected behavior of the user u_i towards the user u_j (multiplied by the sensitivity parameter γ) was positive and the observed behavior was up-voting, we would not create a positive edge, because the observed behavior would not differ from the expected behavior in which no positive discrimination was assumed.

We have computed the distributions of the sensitivity parameter for Models A, B, and C, and for each model and for each type of network (positive and negative) we have computed the threshold of the third tercile. Based on the computed threshold we have created final networks N_1^A, N_1^B, and N_1^C. The final parameters of these networks are presented in Table 1.

Table 1. Parameters of networks

type	name	γ	vertices	edges
positive	N_0^+		56 565	2 927 050
negative	N_0^-		29 403	410 081
positive	N_1^{A+}	0.9369	44 633	2 141 613
negative	N_1^{A-}	0.155	26 869	326 042
positive	N_1^{B+}	0.9397	43 793	2 137 190
negative	N_1^{B-}	0.1613	26 871	325 693
positive	N_1^{C+}	0.8988	44 519	1 981 127
negative	N_1^{C-}	0.0914	25 898	314 942
negative	N_2^C		24 644	312 053

After building the networks, we have decided to measure several popular SNA metrics and compare the results obtained from the baseline network with results obtained from more sophisticated models. We have decided to use the following metrics [8]:

- *modularity*: it measures how many edges connect nodes belonging to a group within the network as compared to the expected number of edges if these edges were created randomly, modularity is often used as a convenient measure of clustering of the network into tightly connected sub-networks.
- *clustering coefficient*: the local clustering coefficient of a node is the ratio of the number of existing edges in the ego-network of a node to the number of all possible edges in the ege-network, this local measure is often averaged over all nodes belonging to the network and reported as a single measure of the density of connections within the network.
- *average network degree*: this measure simply reports the average number of edges a node has in the network, it is practically useless in networks where the degree distribution is governed by the power laws, but nevertheless it is often measured and used as a descriptive quality of a network.
- *network diameter*: the diameter of the network, also known as the maximum eccentricity of the network, is the greatest distance between any pair of nodes within the network.

- *density*: it measures the ratio of the number of edges existing in the network to the number of all possible edges that could exist in the complete graph.

These measures are often used to describe quantitatively various networks and we were interested in the degree to which the measurements from the baseline model would differ. The results are presented in Tables 2 and 3.

Table 2. Comparison of positive network measurements

measure	N_0^+	N_1^{A+}	Δ	N_1^{B+}	Δ	N_1^{C+}	Δ	error
modularity	0.263	0.24	9.5%	0.241	9.1%	0.236	11.4%	10%
clustering coeff.	0.136	0.122	11.4%	0.117	16%	0.101	34.6%	20.6%
average degree	51.74	47.94	7.9%	48.80	6%	44.50	16.2%	10%
diameter	12	11	9%	11	9%	12	0%	6%
density	0.001	0.001	0%	0.001	0%	0.001	0%	0%

Table 3. Comparison of negative network measurements

measure	N_0^-	N_1^{A-}	Δ	N_1^{B-}	Δ	N_1^{C-}	Δ	N_2^{C}	Δ	error
modularity	0.263	0.256	2.7%	0.253	3.9%	0.251	4.7%	0.248	6%	4.3%
clustering coeff.	0.035	0.031	12.9%	0.03	16.6%	0.024	45.8%	0.025	40%	28.8%
average degree	13.95	12.13	14.9%	12.12	15%	12.16	14.6%	12.66	10.1%	13.6%
diameter	11	10	10%	10	10%	10	10%	10	10%	10%
density	0	0	0%	0	0%	0	0%	0.001	0%	0%

As we can see, both for positive and negative networks the naive approach of network construction produces structures that have over-estimated and highly skewed parameters. The average error of estimation for positive networks varies from 6% for network diameter, to 20% for the clustering coefficient. Density estimation seems not to be affected, but this is caused only by the extreme low values of density for these networks. Similarly, in negative networks estimation of parameters can be skewed from 4% in case of modularity, up to 29% for clustering coefficient. Even the average node degree can be miscalculated by over 13% when only the naive approach is taken. These results show clearly that in order to achieve high quality of measurement of collaborative work environments, a special care must be taken to correctly understand the semantics of the underlying relationships before constructing the network.

6   Conclusions

In this paper we have examined the conditions of measuring varying network parameters in social networks representing online collaboration environments. We have focused on the behaviors of users of an online news aggregation service. Our premise was that a naive approach of automatic edge creation (both positive and negative) whenever a slightest sign of behavior is present may lead to highly skewed results. To counteract this phenomenon we have introduced three probabilistic models of user behavior in an online news aggregation service, and based on our models we have constructed more detailed and accurate networks. After repeating the measurements on the new network we have found that various network parameters can be incorrectly computed and sometimes with gross over-estimations, reaching almost 30% in case of the clustering coefficient.

We believe that these primary experiments will convince social network analysis and mining practitioners to be more careful in constructing their networks. Our main contribution is the confirmation of the bias present in network measurements when too many apparent relationships are turned into real-world relationships. By comparing the actual behavior of users with the assumed model in which the null hypothesis states that no discrimination is present between the users, we see that there are significant differences between expected and observed behaviors. This, in turn, supports our claim that the true network consists of these relationships, which invalidate the "no discrimination" assumption.

References

1. Brass, D.J., Butterfield, K.D., Skaggs, B.C.: Relationships and unethical behavior: A social network perspective. Academy of Management Review 23(1), 14–31 (1998)
2. Brzozowski, M.J., Hogg, T., Szabo, G.: Friends and foes: ideological social networking. In: Proceedings of the SIGCHI Conference on Human Factors in Computing Systems, pp. 817–820. ACM (2008)
3. Cartwright, D., Harary, F.: Structural balance: a generalization of heider's theory. Psychological Review 63(5), 277 (1956)
4. Heider, F.: The psychology of interpersonal relations. Psychology Press (2013)
5. Kunegis, J., Lommatzsch, A., Bauckhage, C.: The slashdot zoo: mining a social network with negative edges. In: Proceedings of the 18th International Conference on World Wide Web, pp. 741–750. ACM (2009)
6. Labianca, G., Brass, D.J.: Exploring the social ledger: Negative relationships and negative asymmetry in social networks in organizations. Academy of Management Review 31(3), 596–614 (2006)
7. Leskovec, J., Huttenlocher, D., Kleinberg, J.: Predicting positive and negative links in online social networks. In: Proceedings of the 19th International Conference on World Wide Web, pp. 641–650. ACM (2010)
8. Wasserman, S.: Social network analysis: Methods and applications, vol. 8. Cambridge University Press (1994)

What Makes a Good Team of Wikipedia Editors? A Preliminary Statistical Analysis

Leszek Bukowski[1], Michał Jankowski-Lorek[1], Szymon Jaroszewicz[2,3], and Marcin Sydow[1,3,*]

[1] Polish-Japanese Institute of Information Technology
Koszykowa 86, 02-008 Warsaw, Poland
[2] National Institute of Telecommunications
Szachowa 1, 04-894 Warsaw, Poland
[3] Institute of Computer Science, Polish Academy of Sciences
Jana Kazimierza 5, 01-248 Warsaw, Poland
{bqpro,fooky}@pjwstk.edu.pl,
s.jaroszewicz@ipipan.waw.pl, msyd@poljap.edu.pl

Abstract. The paper concerns studying the quality of teams of Wikipedia authors with statistical approach. We report preparation of a dataset containing numerous behavioural and structural attributes and its subsequent analysis and use to predict team quality. We have performed exploratory analysis using partial regression to remove the influence of attributes not related to the team itself. The analysis confirmed that the key issue significantly influencing article's quality are discussions between teem members. The second part of the paper successfully uses machine learning models to predict good articles based on features of the teams that created them.

Keywords: team quality, Wikipedia, dataset, statistical data mining.

1 Introduction

This paper concerns the problem of quality of Wikipedia editor teams. More precisely, we report a recent work on a set of attributes computed on a real data concerning Wikipedia team quality.

We report *preparation of a dataset* containing numerous *behavioural* and *structural* attributes computed on a real collaboration network downloaded from Wikipedia. Some attributes were reported in other works before, but, up to our knowledge, the whole set of attributes reported here was not studied before in such a context. The presented dataset is a substantial extension of an earlier existing one and is to be made publicly available for other researchers at http://wikitems.pjwstk.edu.pl/data.

Subsequently we report *preliminary statistical analysis* of this data and preliminary results concerning application of machine learning to *predict* the quality of a Wikipedia article.

* This work is supported by Polish National Science Centre grant 2012/05/B/ST6/03364.

A. Nadamoto et al. (Eds.): SocInfo 2013 Workshops, LNCS 8359, pp. 14–28, 2014.

Since there are available huge amounts of logged edit data concerning the work of contributors to Wikipedia articles it is interesting to apply data mining techniques to get some insights into this process. It is reasonable to expect that as a long-term goal of the preliminary research presented here , some phenomena observed in one dataset will be also present in other data, so that they would form some *universal laws*. Detecting such laws would be very valuable to improve the quality of social media and to understand some *sociological* aspects of the analysed processes.

The authors hope that the work presented in this paper would serve as one of the initial steps on a long way to achieve such goals.

One of the additional contributions of our paper is that we take into account correlations between variables such that the influence of variables strictly related to the team is isolated from variables influenced primarily by aspects such as article popularity. We show that such confounding variables can significantly distort the picture and present some techniques to tackle this problem in order to obtain more meaningful results.

1.1 Related Work

Social Network Analysis (SNA) have been used as a framework for study communities of Wikipedia editors. Behavioural social networks have been widely used to model the knowledge community of Wikipedia editors. Such networks are derived from observed behaviour that has been (in the case of Wikipedia) recorded in the edit history. Especially multi-dimensional (multi-layered) social network (MDSN) model [8] of Wikipedia knowledge community is a useful tool for practical applications, such as recommender systems of editors, admin candidates, and for specialised applications, such as conflict detection or evaluating article quality. For example in [12,10,4] researchers have been using network structure as a model of conflict and collaboration between editors. According to balanced networks theory [17] in such situations, when conflict arises in social network, actors shall form densely connected clusters of collaborators, who are conflicted with actors from other clusters.

Conflict and collaboration are not the only topics that have been analysed with SNA techniques. Another problem that attracts significant attention is the problem of coordination [9,10]: one of the main phenomenon that is associated with Wikipedia is that all articles and entries have been created by teams of editors without any central authority. For example in [9] it has been shown that adding more editors to an article might improve article quality only when appropriate coordination techniques are used. Another work that examines problems surrounding coordination and conflict in Wikipedia is [11].

We are not aware of previous research that isolates team-related features from other confounding aspects such as article popularity.

In [16,15], social network analysis was performed on the behavioural social network mined from the entire edit history since the inception of Polish Wikipedia in 2001. This paper partially builds on that work.

The machine learning approach to predict trust in social networks was studied in [2] and [3]. Similar analysis of usability of various attributes but in the domain of web spam prediction is presented in [13].

2 Data

We significantly extended our previous MDSN dataset mentioned earlier [15].

The MDSN data is a multi-graph, where the set of nodes A consists of the Wikipedia authors and the arcs fall into several behavioural categories (dimensions). : *co-edits*, *reverts* and *discussions*, that will be described later.

In this paper, we assume that for each Wikipedia article its *team* is the set of all the authors whose contributions are present in the final version of the article (at the moment of collecting the data). For each article, the nodes representing such authors induce a subgraph for which we computed various attributes. While one might argue that such a definition is a bit simplistic, it is quite natural and intuitive. [1]

When computing the attributes in this paper, the dimensions are never combined, i.e. each attribute is derived from exactly one of the dimensions.

In this paper, for each team we consider and compute a large number (almost 100) of attributes to be subsequently used in statistical analysis of the data. The attributes can be divided into two groups: behavioural and purely graph-based, that will be described in detail in next subsections. Some attributes are very technical and hard to be naturally interpreted, especially the "triad-based" ones. The approach of making the initial number of potential attributes large is typical in machine learning and makes it possible to avoid omitting any piece of information that may turn out to be useful in analysis or prediction. Subsequent analysis will indicate which attributes are actually useful, the remainder may be eventually dropped.

In addition, we assign each article a decision variable called `featured` that represents the fact whether it is a high-quality article. The variable is set to `TRUE` iff the article was marked as "featured" or "good" in Wikipedia. This decision variable will be treated as a gold-standard in our subsequent statistical analysis.

2.1 Behavioural Attributes

Chosen behavioral attributes utilize the available data in Wikipedia edit history. These attributes try to approximate significant social concepts, such as acquaintance, trust, distrust, that can have an impact on teamwork. For more detailed attribute explanation, see [15].

For each pair of authors $(a_1, a_2) \in A^2$ in the same team, there potentially exist three directed arcs between them, each corresponding to one of the behavioural dimensions. The arcs have non-negative weights that are computed as follows.

---

[1] Furtermore it was inherited from the initial dataset that is being extended in this paper. We plan to make the team definition more sophisticated in our ongoing work.

Co-edits is defined as the amount of text (number of words) written by one author next to the text of other author invertedly weighted by the word distance between them.

$$coedits(a_1, a_2) = \sum_{(w_1, w_2)} 1/(wordDistance(w_1, w_2))$$

where the summation is taken over all pairs of words in the considered article (w_1, w_2) in each revision, where w_1 is added in the current revision by author a_1 and w_2 had been previously written by a_2 and the word distance is at most $maxWordDistance$, that after some experimentation, was set to 20. The threshold of 20 provides a good balance between computational efficiency and the relevance of the edition.

Reverts describes how many times one author reverted to a revision that is identical to a previous revision of the second author but not further away that $maxRecent$ revisions ago (that we set to 20).

The strength of a *discussion* dimension between two authors of a team counts the number of times when the first author wrote a word after the text of the second author in the same article or user talk page but not further away than discussionDistance (that we set to 20 words).

Abbreviations *disc* (or *discussion*) as well as *rev* or *edit* will be used as parts of attribute names later in the paper.

Next, for subgraph induced by each team T and for each dimension, we *aggregated* all the weights of arcs in this subgraph in three ways: as *sum*, sum normalised by the number of arcs in the subgraph (called *avge*) and sum normalised by the maximum potential number of edges in that graph $|T|(|T| - 1)$ (called *avgv*). These abbreviations are used as suffixes in names of corresponding attributes mentioned later in this paper. For example, discussion_avge, etc.

We have created 300 069 subgraphs for all teams based on MDSN and then calculated 23 attributes for each MDSN dimension.

In addition, some other attributes have been computed for each team, for example: *edits* (total number of edits made to the article), *anon_edits* (number of edits made by anonymous users), *bot_edits* (number of edits when the username contained the "bot" as a suffix), etc.

2.2 Structural Attributes

Based on the MSDN network, we additionally computed numerous attributes that are based on pure structural properties of the underlying graph. The attributes are as follows. The abbreviations in brackets will be later used in attribute names mentioned later in this paper (e.g. *rev_nodc* stands for out-degree centrality computed on the *revisions* dimension, etc.)

- network in-degree centralisation (*nidc*)
- network out-degree centralisation (*nodc*)
- betweenness centralisation (*nbc*)
- number of week components (*nwcc*)

- size of the largest week component (*solwcc*)
- number of strong components (*nscc*)
- size of the largest strong component (*solscc*)
- triadic census (16 variables describing each triad tr_i for $i \in \{1, 2, 3...16\}$)

In-degree and *out-degree centrality* (also known as, simply, in-degree and out-degree) of a *single node* are the number of incoming and outcoming arcs, respectively.

E.g. the in-degree of some author x in the dimension of *co-edits* reflects the number of other authors that have edited the text near x's texts. Respectively the out-degree of x reflects the number of other authors near whose text x has edited. We also do such computations for reverts and discussion dimensions.

The *in-degree centralisation of a whole graph* G is the variation of in-degree centrality of nodes from G divided by the maximum possible variation of in-degrees in a network of the size G. It is given by the following formula:

$$C_G^{in} = \sum_{i=1}^{n} (d_{in-max}(G) - d_{in}(v_i))/(n-1)^2 \qquad (1)$$

Where n is the total number of nodes in G; $d_{in}(v_i)$ is the in-degree of the i-th node in G and $d_{in-max}(G)$ is the highest observed in-degree in G. Metric C_G^{in} is always 1 for the networks where there is just one node to which all other nodes send ties – i. e. C_G^{in} is equal 1 in all networks, where $d_{in}(v^*) = (n-1)$ and for all other nodes $d_{in}(v_i) = 0$. The fact that maximal possible value of in-degrees variation in a network of size n is equal $(n-1)^2$ might be explained as follows: when all nodes send relations to just one node, then we have to $n-1$ times sum up $(n-1) - 0$, so it is just $(n-1)(n-1)$, which equals $(n-1)^2$.

C_G^{out} is defined analogously.

Betweenness centrality of a node v_i in a digraph is given by:

$$C_B(v_i) = \sum_{j<k} p_{jk}(v_i)/p_{jk} \qquad (2)$$

Where $p_{jk}(v_i)$ is the number of the shortest paths between nodes j and k, that pass through node v_i and p_{jk} is the number of all the shortest paths between j and k. The maximum of equation (2) is $[(n-1)(n-2)]$, which is the number of all directed pairs in the network not including v_i. So in digraphs $C_B(v_i)$ is normalised as follows:

$$C_B'(v_i) = C_B(v_i)/[(n-1)(n-2)] \qquad (3)$$

Based on the above, the *betweenness centralisation for a given network* G is defined as follows:

$$C_G^B = \sum_{i=1}^{n} (C_B'(v^*) - C_B'(v_i))/(n-1) \qquad (4)$$

By $C'_B(v^*)$ we mean the highest betweenness centrality observed in G, normalised according to formula (3). The value of C_G^B is 1 in the networks where all the shortest paths, that would possibly pass through just one particular node, in fact pass trough that node and for all other nodes $C_B(v_i) = 0$, so there are no shortest paths that pass through them.

We also count the number of *connected components* for each network. A *weakly connected component* of a network G is a maximal such a subgraph of G so that for each pair of nodes in G there exists a path in G between them while the directions of the arcs can be ignored. A *strongly connected component* is defined similarly, but the path has to be directed.

2.3 Triads

In case of digraphs, that represent some social networks, we can investigate of how many *triads* of a certain kind they include.

Triads are the triplets of actors who might interact somehow with each other. These interactions are represented by arcs. There are 16 possible configurations that any triple of actors from a digraph might be in. Starting from an empty triad (003), where there are no arcs between any two nodes and ending in a complete triad, where all possible arcs are present (300). All triads might be identified by so called "M-A-N number" which is a three-digit number, sometimes supported by additional letter. The first digit indicates how many mutual dyads exist in a triad in question; that is how many pairs of nodes are in configurations where choices are reciprocated. The second digit indicates how many asymmetric dyads one can find in the triad under consideration. Finally, the last digit informs how many null dyads exist in the given triad – null dyads are pairs of actors between

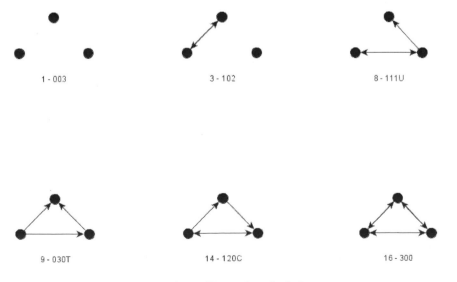

Fig. 1. Examples of triads

whom there are no arcs. For example, we can see on Figure 1, that the triad where there are no arcs between nodes is coded as 003. Respectively, the triad number 9 on the picture is coded as 030T: indeed it includes just three asymmetric dyads and it is transitive, so we have a letter "T".

We may test some structural hypothesis about networks in questions by investigating the frequencies of occurrence of some types of triads. The simplest situation is so called "balanced network", where all actors form just two clusters between which there are no interactions. Think for example about a conflicted group of people, who have formed two factions and they collaborate only with the members of their own group. For simplicity, assume that choices are always reciprocated. In such a network there would be only two types of triads – namely: 102 and 300. Indeed no matter which triplet of actors you choose from that network, they have to be in one of these two configurations: 102 or 300 – or it is the case that all three actors are in the same faction (300) or just two of them is in one party, and the third one is in the opposite faction (102).

Obviously, perfectly balanced networks are very rare in empirical studies. It is much more convenient to compare the empirical distributions of some types of triads with their expected distributions, which are computed under assumption, that the networks in question have been generated by some random, stochastic process. For example, if we investigate some social network, where arcs between actors represent trust, then we might expect, that there is a tendency towards transitivity in that network. So if actor i trusts j and j trusts k, then we might expect, that there is an arc from i to k. In such a network all triads, that are transitive – i. e. that contain a following configuration $i \rightarrow j \quad and \quad j \rightarrow k \quad and \quad i \rightarrow k$ – should be more frequent, than in a random network consisting of the same actors. In figure 1 all three bottom triads are transitive.

3   Exploratory Analysis

In this section we present an exploratory analysis of the data. We include all available variables and use statistical analysis to discover previously unknown relationships between those variables and the team quality.

As the pre-processing step, we removed teams with less than 15 members. The reason was that social network analysis measures such as triads are not meaningful for such small networks. Next, we replaced all attributes with their logarithms (one was added before taking logarithms to avoid taking logarithms of zero) in order to correct a significant skew present in the distributions of almost all variables. After the transformations, the data consisted of 38208 records with 89 attributes. Out of all articles, only 0.9% were marked as 'good' or 'featured', the class distribution is therefore highly imbalanced.

3.1   Initial Analysis

ROC curves [6] are a popular method of assessing the performance of classification models. It depicts the tradeoff between the percentage of positive cases identified by the model (y-axis) and the percentage of incorrectly labeled negative cases. The curve is frequently summarized with a single number: the Area Under the ROC Curve abbreviated AUC. The ROC curve is diagonal for a random model with AUC equal to 0.5, for a perfect predictor the curve passes through the point $(0, 1)$ and the AUC is equal to 1. AUC is equal to 0 for a model which always predicts the opposite class. Notice that such a model can easily be converted into a perfect predictor by reversing its scores.

We first look at how predictive each attribute is. Instead of using traditional measures for evaluating attribute usefulness, we use the AUC measure of single attribute models. This allows us to easily compare single attributes with more complicated models.

To this end, we treat each attribute as a predictive model and draw ROC curves for this model. For each attribute, its area under the ROC curve (AUC) is used to assess the predictiveness. Recall that highly predictive attributes have AUC close either to 0 or to 1 so we use $\max\{AUC, 1 - AUC\}$ as the final measure.

In the following when we talk about AUC we are in fact referring to this quantity.

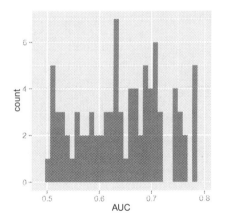

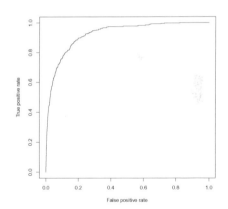

Fig. 2. Distribution of AUCs for attributes in the initial dataset

Fig. 3. ROC curve for logistic regression model built on the original variables

Figure 2 shows the distribution of AUCs for all attributes. It can be seen than many attributes are predictive with the median AUC being 0.641.

The most predictive attribute was `disc_nidc` with an AUC of 0.785. Other most predictive attributes were also related to the discussion dimension.

Afterwards we computed a logistic regression model on all available variables. The model was highly predictive, its ROC curve is shown in Figure 3. Coefficients of several attributes had p-values close to 0 with the most significant attribute being the `edits` attribute: total number of editions made to the article.

This immediately shows the following problem with an approach that has been taken by most previous research: article quality depends on the amount of

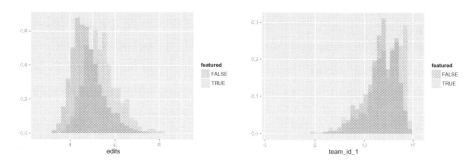

Fig. 4. Histograms within both classes for the `edits` and `team_id_1` attributes

work devoted to it and this in turn is related to aspects such as article popularity which are *not* the qualities of the team per se. Moreover, the risk is that other attributes are predictive not because they measure team quality, but because they are correlated with the total amount of work devoted to the article. The correlation of `edits` with `disc_nidc` the variable with the highest AUC is in fact quite low (0.08), but its correlation with the second most predictive variable `disc_tr_16` was 0.53, indeed fairly high.

Figure 4 (left) shows the histogram of the logarithm of the total number of edits within both classes. One can see that higher number of edits favours the situation that the resulting article is "good". This attribute is a confounder since it is not a property of the team itself. Later, this will be further discussed.

An interesting observation is that the `team_id_1` attribute is also quite informative (AUC=0.602). The interpretation is that `team_id_1` is (invertedly) correlated to the age of the article, so the higher `team_id_1` the later first version of the article was created. Collective experience of all Wikipedia users is growing so that number of good articles is rising with time. Other interpretation might be that increased rate of good articles in time is due to the popularity of new topics and new way of promoting it for example through "article of the day".

3.2 Eliminating the Confounding Variables

There are several techniques available in statistical literature which allow for removing the effect of controlling variables [7]. The easiest is to keep a slice of the data small enough for the values of all such variables to be approximately constant. This amounts to conditioning on the confounding variables thus removing their influence. Typically, the analysis is performed by conditioning on several different values of the confounding variables. Special provisions exist in statistical packages e.g. for drawing regression plots for various conditioning values [7].

Note that simply removing the confounding variables is not sufficient, as they are correlated with the remaining attributes. For this reason, attribute selection is not sufficient, and we use partial regression techniques instead.

The advantage of conditioning is that it works correctly when the variables to be cancelled influence the remaining ones nonlinearly. Unfortunately, the method leads to severe data loss, and is thus in practice limited to conditioning on one or two variables. In the problem at hand the percentage of featured articles is quite small so the technique is not suitable.

Another approach, which we are going to use in this paper, are partial regression methods [7]. The idea is to build regression models which predict all variables in the dataset based on the confounding ones. The confounding variables are then removed and all remaining variables are replaced with *residuals* from regressions on the confounders. Recall that the residuals in a linear model are the differences between the true and predicted values, and that they are uncorrelated (see e.g. [14]) with the predictor variables (confounders in our case). As a result, after the transformation, the resulting variables are uncorrelated with the ones whose influence we are trying to eliminate.

The advantage of this method is that it avoids the data loss incurred by conditioning; the disadvantage, that the removal of confounding is only as good as the regression models used. The method is typically applied in the classical, linear regression setting. The differences between the two approaches are investigated (for the case of partial and conditional correlation) e.g. in [1].

Due to the problems with data loss incurred by conditioning we have used partial regression techniques to analyze our data. First, we remove the influence of the total number of edits applied to an article and the article id. To this end we build linear regression models from `edits` and `team_id_1` to all other variables in the dataset except the predicted variable `featured`. The two variables are then removed and all others replaced with residuals of their respective model. Notice that as a result all variables become *uncorrelated* with the total number of edits and article id. Recall that the class attribute has not been affected. Replacing it with appropriate residuals would lead to overly optimistic results as uncertainty caused by removing the confounders would also be removed.

After taking those steps we repeated the analysis from Section 3.1. Overall, the variables became much less predictive, the median AUC for separate variables went down from 0.641 to 0.587. This confirms that the true cause for predictiveness of several variables lied in them being correlated with the total number of work done on the article by the team.

After conditioning, the AUC of the most predictive attribute `disc_nidc` went down from 0.785 to 0.774, a very small decrease. However, as the next section shows, other confounding variables still need to be removed, which will more significantly decrease the predictive value of this attribute.

3.3 Anonymous Edits

Interestingly, the new most predictive attribute was `anon_edits` which gives the total number of anonymous edits. Its AUC was 0.812. Figure 5 (left) shows the histogram of the values of the attribute (actually the residuals obtained by projecting them onto the removed attributes).

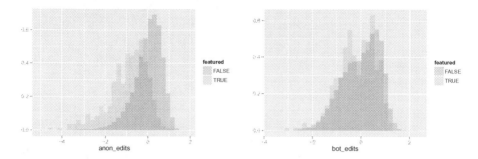

Fig. 5. Histograms of the total number of anonymous and bot edits conditioned on the total amount of work spent on an article. Note that the x axis represents the residuals from projecting the plotted variables onto `edits` and `team_id_1`.

One can observe that the general phenomenon that the more anonymous edits the worse quality of the article. It might be interpreted on a psychological background as follows. When a user makes an edit under an overt id she engages more and tries to do their best to make the edit of the best possible quality since it can be publicly assessed by the community and influences the overall user reputation. Anononymous edit, instead, does not put such a responsibility on the editing user.

The right-hand side of the figure shows the analogous histogram for the related `bot_edits` attribute which does not show such predictive power (AUC of 0.57). This confirms that anonymous edits are in a way special.

The number of anonymous edits may be partly related to the team itself, but we do not have any measures that would isolate such relationship from aspects such as how controversial a given topic is. We have thus decided to remove the attribute (and the `bot_edits` as well) by conditioning on it in the partial regression approach.

3.4 Variables Directly Related to the Team Performance

After conditioning on the numbers of anonymous and bot edits, the AUC of individual variables has decreased further, the median being equal to 0.540. Most variables are no longer predictive, which confirms that their correlations with the class variables were spurious and resulted mainly from being correlated with other, more predictive variables.

The five most predictive variables are `disc_nscc` (AUC=0.687), `disc_nidc` (AUC=0.681), `disc_nwcc` (AUC=0.671), `disc_nodc` (AUC=0.671) and `disc_avgv` (AUC=0.640). Figure 6 shows the histograms and ROC curves for those attributes. The plots are of course made *after* removing the influence of the total number of edits, team id, and the total numbers of anonymous and bot edits. Recall that when the AUC is less than 0.5 a better predictor can be obtained by reversing the scores. The first and third curves are thus reversed (this is the case since a large number of connected components means a weakly connected network).

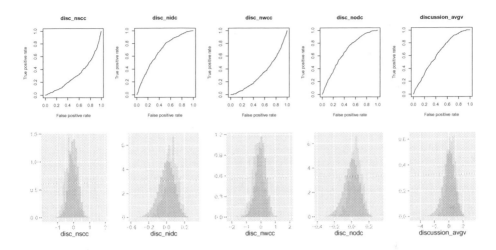

Fig. 6. Histograms and ROC curves for variables describing the discussion dimension of the Multidimensional Social Network. Note that the x axis of the histograms represents the residuals from projecting the plotted variables onto the removed variables.

It can be seen that the discussion dimension is very important. The average (thus corrected for the team size) number of discussions is highly, positively, correlated with article quality.

Unfortunately all those variables are correlated (minimum correlation between them is 0.46) thus it may be difficult to isolate the influence of specific, network-related, aspects of the discussion dimension. This is confirmed after removing the influence of the `disc_nscc` attribute in the next section.

3.5   Further Analysis

To see if any other dimensions influence article quality we added the `disc_nscc` attribute to the list of attributes on which we project in our partial regression procedure. All discussion-related variables lost their prominence and the most predictive variables were those related to the reverts dimension.

The most predictive attribute with AUC of 0.634 was `reverts_avgv` with negative values promoting better articles. It may be interpreted that if there is much mutual coordination (little reverts) between the authors then the resulting article is good.

After removing the influence of `reverts_avgv` the various attributes related to discussion, co-edits and reverts dimensions were the top predictors, but the picture became less clear and their AUCs were only about 0.6. We have thus decided that we have reached the limits of the current methods and stopped the exploratory analysis here.

4 Prediction

In this section we attempt to predict team quality based on all available variables after, however, removing the influence of the total number of edits, team id and the percentage of anonymous and bot edits. To this end we replace the original dataset with the dataset used in partial regression with controlling for those four attributes. Afterwards, several machine-learning models are built on the dataset and their predictive power is examined.

To accurately assess model peformance while taking overfitting into account we have split the data into two separate training and test sets of equal sizes. The models are built on the training set and evaluated on the test set.

We have used a representative selection of machine learning methods.

In particular, we have used the logistic regression model and the CART [5] decision tree learner implemented in the R statistical package in the rpart package. When building decision trees records from the more frequent class (not-featured) have been assigned lower weights to balance the distribution of the classes. Additionally, we used three machine learning methods from the Weka program: boosted decision trees (the AdaBoost.M1 algorithm), Random Forest, and the naive Bayesian classifier with kernel estimation for numerical attributes. We used 50 iterations of the AdaBoost.M1 and Random Forest algorithms.

Figure 7 shows the ROC curves for all those models. It can be seen that AdaBoost turned out to be the best model for the task. The area under the ROC curve for this model was 0.7965, dramatically higher than for any single attribute. Recall that in Section 3.4 the most predictive attribute disc_nscc achieved the AUC of only 0.687.

The results demonstrate that using different attributes as inputs to a predictive model can be a highly successful technique for team assessment. Recall that we have used partial regression techniques to remove the influence of attributes related mainly to the article and not the team itself (e.g. topic popularity).

4.1 Predictive Power of Various Groups of Attributes

Next we proceed to assessing predictive power of various types of variables in order to determine which factors are most useful in predicting team qaulity. To this end we have build predictive models on four subsets of variables and compared their performance. We began by using the AdaBoost model here as, in the previous experiment, it offered the best peformance.

The attributes were divided into three sets: behavioural (Section 2.1), structural excluding triads (Section 2.2) and triads (Section 2.3).

All models reported in this section included the behavioural attributes being the basic descriptors of features from which other attributes are derived. The Area Under the ROC Curve of an AdaBoost model containing only behavioural attributes was 0.6522, i.e. much lower than for the full model (0.7965). Next we added the structural attributes achieving AUC of 0.7254. A model using behavioural attributes and triads reached the AUC of 0.77 still lower than the full model. It is thus clear that network structure variables offer some potential

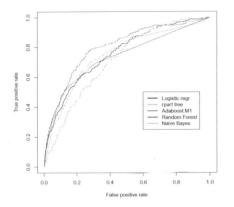
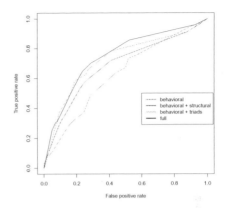

Fig. 7. ROC curves for models predicting the quality of teams of Wikipedia editors

Fig. 8. ROC curves for CART decission tree models build on various subsets of variables

predictive power beyond that offered by the behavioural variables introduced in [15] and using a combination of different types of team features in a predictive model is highly beneficial.

Next we have repeated the analysis for CART decision trees obtaining similar results. The basic behavioural variables achieved only AUC of 0.6273. Adding non-triad based structure variables increased the AUC to 0.6847. The model based on the basic behavioural variables and triads achieved an AUC of 0.7239. The full model including both types of attributes had AUC 0.7463. Figure 8 shows the ROC curves for the four models.

5   Conclusions

Reported results give some initial insights into the process of preparing a good Wikipedia article. It is demonstrated that applicaton of some appropriate statistical techniques helps to reveal some less obvious phenomena. Also, both behavioural and structural attributes seem to contribute to the resulting teamwork quality. The main contribution of this article is to demonstrate that while team size and number of edits have the strongest impact on Wikipedia article quality, it is possible to consider other, team related features that are also significant. We demonstrate this significance by using statistical techniques that allow to evaluate these weaker features in the presence of stronger ones. We find that attributes derived from the behavioral social network based on article discussion (talk pages) have a significant impact on article quality. In open teams, it is not always possible to increase the number of actively participating team members, or to increase the level of activity of existing members. Wikipedia editors are self-motivated. Yet, sometimes it may be possible to better organize the contributions of existing team members. This is the main future direction of our research.

References

1. Baba, K., Shibata, R., Sibuya, M.: Partial correlation and conditional correlation as measures of conditional independence. Australian & New Zealand Journal of Statistics 46(4), 657–664 (2004)
2. Borzymek, P., Sydow, M.: Trust and distrust prediction in social network with combined graphical and review-based attributes. In: Jędrzejowicz, P., Nguyen, N.T., Howlet, R.J., Jain, L.C. (eds.) KES-AMSTA 2010, Part I. LNCS, vol. 6070, pp. 122–131. Springer, Heidelberg (2010)
3. Borzymek, P., Sydow, M., Wierzbicki, A.: Enriching trust prediction model in social network with user rating similarity. In: Wegrzyn-Wolska, K., Abraham, A., Snasel, V. (eds.) Proceedings of the 1st International Conference on Computational Aspects of Social Networks (CASoN 2009), pp. 40–47. IEEE Computer Society, Los Alamitos (2009)
4. Brandes, U., Lerner, J.: Visual analysis of controversy in user-generated encyclopedias. Information Visualization 7(1), 34–48 (2008)
5. Brieman, L., Friedman, J.H., Olshen, R.A., Stone, C.J.: Classification and regression trees (1984)
6. Fawcett, T.: An introduction to roc analysis. Pattern Recogn. Lett. 27(8), 861–874 (2006)
7. Fox, J., Weisberg, S.: An R Companion to Applied Regression. Sage (2011)
8. Kazienko, P., Musial, K., Kukla, E., Kajdanowicz, T., Bródka, P.: Multidimensional social network: Model and analysis. In: Jędrzejowicz, P., Nguyen, N.T., Hoang, K. (eds.) ICCCI 2011, Part I. LNCS, vol. 6922, pp. 378–387. Springer, Heidelberg (2011)
9. Kittur, A., Kraut, R.E.: Harnessing the wisdom of crowds in wikipedia: quality through coordination. In: Proceedings of the 2008 ACM Conference on Computer Supported Cooperative Work, pp. 37–46. ACM (2008)
10. Kittur, A., Kraut, R.E.: Beyond wikipedia: coordination and conflict in online production groups. In: Proceedings of the 2010 ACM Conference on Computer Supported Cooperative Work, CSCW 2010, pp. 215–224. ACM, NY (2010)
11. Kittur, A., Suh, B., Pendleton, B.A., Chi, E.H.: He says, she says: Conflict and coordination in wikipedia. In: Proceedings of the SIGCHI Conference on Human Factors in Computing Systems, CHI 2007, pp. 453–462. ACM, New York (2007)
12. Le, M.-T., Dang, H.-V., Lim, E.-P., Datta, A.: Wikinetviz: Visualizing friends and adversaries in implicit social networks. In: IEEE International Conference on Intelligence and Security Informatics, ISI 2008, pp. 52–57. IEEE (2008)
13. Piskorski, J., Sydow, M., Weiss, D.: Exploring linguistic features for web spam detection: a preliminary study. In: AIRWeb 2008: Proceedings of the 4th International Workshop on Adversarial Information Retrieval on the Web, pp. 25–28. ACM, New York (2008)
14. Rao, C.R., Toutenburg, H.: Linear Models and Generalizations: Least Squares and Alternatives. Springer (2007)
15. Turek, P., Wierzbicki, A., Nielek, R., Hupa, A., Datta, A.: Learning about the quality of teamwork from wikiteams. In: Proceedings of the 2010 IEEE Second International Conference on Social Computing, SocialCom/IEEE International Conference on Privacy, Security, Risk and Trust, PASSAT 2010, Minneapolis, pp. 17–24 (2010)
16. Turek, P., Wierzbicki, A., Nielek, R., Hupa, A., Datta, A.: Wikiteams: How do they achieve success? IEEE Potentials 30(5), 2–7 (2011)
17. Wasserman, S.: Social network analysis: Methods and applications, vol. 8. Cambridge University Press (1994)

iPoster: A Collaborative Browsing Platform for Presentation Slides Based on Semantic Structure

Yuanyuan Wang, Kota Tomoyasu, and Kazutoshi Sumiya

Graduate School of Human Science and Environment, University of Hyogo, Japan
{ne11u001,nd13y015}@stshse.u-hyogo.ac.jp, sumiya@shse.u-hyogo.ac.jp

Abstract. Coursera and SlideShare are crucial platforms for improving education; students are able to obtain various educational presentation materials through the Web. Recently, Prezi introduced a zoomable canvas as a substitute to the traditional presentations that allows users to zoom in and out of the presentation media. Teachers then attempt to provide presentations in a nonlinear fashion for enhancing the user interaction through these presentations. However, creation of non-linear presentations would be time-consuming, besides posing design challenges. In this paper, in order to support collaborative browsing, we build a novel collaborative browsing platform that generates meaningfully structured presentations, called "iPoster;" this enables users to automatically navigate through the slide-based educational materials. The system places elements such as text and graphics of presentation slides in a structural layout by semantically analyzing the slide structure. The structural layout can reveal the hierarchy of elements by moving from the overview to a detail using automatic transitions, such as zooms and pans. Through this, the collaborative browsing platform can support multiple students to interactively browse an iPoster in cyberspace on their tablets. The navigation information maps each student's specific needs by considering the student's operations, and detects other students who have similar learning purposes to help them share their interests with each other.

1   Introduction

Slide-based visual presentation support, such as Microsoft PowerPoint or Apple Keynote, is now one of the most frequently used tools for educational purposes currently. However, this format has been criticized repeatedly because of the limitations it imposes on authors and presenters [16]. Enormous amounts of slide-based educational materials that are often based on the collaborative learning teaching materials (i.e., textbooks), are freely shared on Web sites such as Coursera[1] and SlideShare[2]. Thus, students can browse the presentations anywhere, such as on a public display connected to a computer in a classroom or on their own tablets. However, the current slideshow mode of presentations merely permits fluid navigation of linear structures, even while it is being presented to a

---

[1] https://www.coursera.org/
[2] http://www.slideshare.net/

A. Nadamoto et al. (Eds.): SocInfo 2013 Workshops, LNCS 8359, pp. 29–42, 2014.
© Springer-Verlag Berlin Heidelberg 2014

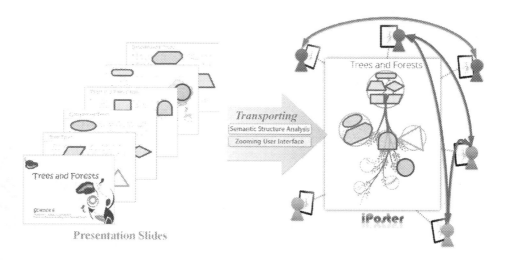

Fig. 1. Conceptual diagram of a collaborative browsing platform based on iPoster

diverse audience. Moreover, in CSCW tools, group awareness plays an important role in enhancing the effectiveness of the application [2]. In a case of a linear text document, it is challenging to map collaborators to one another, based on mutual interests. Canvas presentations are attempts to mitigate the problems posed by slideware. For instance, Prezi[3] provides an infinite canvas with a zoomable user interface (ZUI) [1] as an alternative to the traditional slides. This interface permits the canvas format to support the creation of expressive layouts. These layouts can be zoomed out, allowing the slide arrangement to be presented in its entirety to the audience [8]. The canvas model was also adopted by pptPlex[4]. In order to effectively support collaborative learning, authors and presenters will be required to create and deliver presentations in a nonlinear fashion. However, this will be time-consuming and pose challenges in designing.

As depicted in Fig. 1, we present a collaborative browsing platform that generates a meaningfully structured presentation by transporting the presentation slides. It promotes user interaction and communication and is called the "iPoster," or an interactive poster. Users can access an iPoster on their tablets using a zooming metaphor in cyberspace. They can interactively browse the iPoster through user operations, and connect with each other's tablets. A collaborative browsing platform based on iPoster, which can share and navigate information, matches each user's specific requirements by analyzing the operations of the users. Further, it detects other users who have similar requirements by mapping the similarity in their operations and conveys their interests to each other. iPoster can be implemented by 1) analyzing the semantic structure of textual and graphic elements in slides and the semantic relationships between them; and 2) employing the zooming user interface for organizing elements in

---

[3] http://prezi.com/

[4] http://www.microsoft.com/en-us/download/details.aspx?id=28558

structural layouts, using zooming and panning transitions based on a basic idea of Prezi. In semantic structure analysis, we first extract elements by examining the presentation context of the particular element in the slides. The semantic relationships between these elements are determined using implicit hyperlinks in slides, based on a slide structure. Specifically, we derive the slide structure by focusing on the itemized sentences of bullet points present in the slide text. There are various types of structural layouts for constructing an iPoster, such as tree structure, stacked Venn, and pyramid structure. In this paper, in order to provide an overview of the content, we utilize a tree structure, combined with a stacked Venn for an iPoster. Finally, our iPoster is generated based on semantic relationships, using a ZUI for collaborative browsing, which can raise the collaborative awareness, and interaction, besides enabling users to understand the educational presentations easily and efficiently.

This paper is organized as follows. Section 2 reviews related work. Section 3 describes our semantic structure analysis model to extract elements from slides and to determine the semantic relationships between elements based on the slide structure. Section 4 explains the detailed procedure of an iPoster generation, based on the derived semantic relationships by employing zooming and panning transitions. Section 5 presents our collaborative browsing platform based on iPoster. Finally, Section 6 concludes this paper with suggestions for further work.

2   Related Work

A variety of applications address the identified weaknesses of the current slide-ware tools in the presentation and authoring domains. Our approach in iPoster builds on the strength of collaborative browsing.

Many recent applications address the need to capture complex relationships among content items, and assist in crafting compelling narratives. These applications employ both, new or unusual hardware configurations, as well as novel interfaces. Lanir et al. [5] proposed the MultiPresenter application that leverages spatial reasoning capabilities to relate content through dual-screen projection. Although iPoster does not adopt the dual-audience-display paradigm, it addresses the need to navigate through elements dynamically during the presentation. NextSlidePlease [15] is a novel application for authoring and delivering slideware presentations. This tool addresses issues of content integration, presentation structuring, time-management, and flexible presentation delivery. iPoster is similar to this work, as we utilize a structured layout, rather than one or more slide lists, to allow interactive and collaborative browsing by users for each other.

Good and Bederson [3] proposed replacing the card stack or film strip metaphor with a ZUI in their CounterPoint application, borrowing insights from the domain of mind-maps or concept maps [12] and visual storytelling [11]. Our iPoster uses a ZUI to navigate to the elements from slides. The Fly application addresses graph-based presentation authoring [9]. It provides a set of tools for authoring presentations from scratch in a two-dimensional canvas with defined paths. Our iPoster aims to utilize the strengths of ZUIs for providing an enhanced collaborative browsing tool.

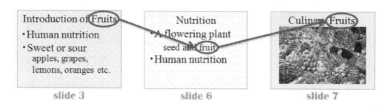

Fig. 2. An example of "fruit" appears at different levels in slides

Maekawa et al. [10] proposed a content partitioning method for collaborative browsing. It converts a tree-structured content into a complete graph and adapts a graph partitioning problem to the graph. On the other hand, Laufer et al. [6] argue about the use of avatars in ZUIs are providing a uniquely efficient environment for collaboration in productivity applications. Multiple users can develop a presentation together; create a mindmap, and a storyline or do brainstorming. Katayama et al. [4] proposed a collaborative document revision system as a web application. The collaborative document revision has a reviser-viewer, a reviser-reviser and a viewer-viewer collaboration. Our collaborative browsing that focuses on users' operations on their tablets using a zooming metaphor.

3   Semantic Structure Analysis of Presentation Slides

In this section, we describe a semantic structure analysis model for extracting elements and determining the semantic relationships between them. Preliminary ideas regarding this model are given in an algebraic query model [13] as well.

3.1   Element Extraction

The two most salient and dominant elements in a presentation slide are the set of textual elements and the set of graphic elements. These are based on the itemized sentences of bullet points in the slide text. We define the slide title as the 1st level, the first item of text within the slide body as the 2nd level, and the depth of the sub-items increases with the indentation levels (3rd level, 4th level, and so on). Non-text objects such as figures or tables are considered to be at the same indention level as the surrounding text.

Textual Elements. We define textual elements as topics that focus on the nouns in slides. Based on the presentation context, a topic can be described as a learning point with multiple nouns that frequently appears at the higher levels (such as in the slide title) in neighboring slides. Initially, we extract noun phrases using a language analysis toolkit MSR Splat[5] based on the XML files of slides.

The topics that appear in the title of a slide and the body of other slides can be considered to indicate its context in a presentation (see Fig. 2). Then, we

---

[5] http://research.microsoft.com/en-us/projects/msrsplat/

extract topics by locating the same noun phrases in different slides, at varied levels. If a noun phrase k appears at different levels in slides s_i and s_j, then k is a candidate for being one of the topics T in the presentation. The steps to determine T using k is explained here, which is presented both, in s_i and s_j.

$$T = \{(k, s_i, s_j)|l_{max}(k, s_i) \neq l_{max}(k, s_j)\} \tag{1}$$

where, T is a bag of noun phrases that can be considered as candidates for topics. $l_{max}(k, s_i)$ is a function that returns the highest level of k in the slide s_i. For instance, when the highest level is the title, i.e., the first indentation level, of s_i, then $l_{max}(k, s_i)$ returns 1; and when the highest level is the third indentation level of s_j, then $l_{max}(k, s_j)$ returns 3. When k appears at different levels, k is determined as a candidate for topics provided $l_{max}(k, s_i)$ is not equal to $l_{max}(k, s_j)$. Then, the weight of k in T is defined using the levels of k, and the distance between slides s_i and s_j, as follows:

$$I(k) = \frac{1}{l_{max}(k, s_i)} + \sum_{k, s_i, s_j \in T} \left(\frac{1}{l_{max}(k, s_j)} \cdot \frac{1}{dist(s_i, s_j)} \right) \tag{2}$$

where $l_{max}(k, s_i)$ indicates the weight of k in s_i, i.e., it returns the highest level of k in slide s_i by Eq. (1). $dist(s_i, s_j)$ corresponds to the strength of the association between s_i and s_j, and it denotes the distance between s_i and s_j. Thus, if k appears at a high level in s_i and s_j, and the distance between s_i and s_j is short, the weight $I(k)$ of k is high. Here, k, s_i, and s_j belong to T in Eq. (1).

Graphic Elements. When compared to pure textual elements, images are more attractive, appealing and informative from a psychological standpoint. Based on the study of search results presentation [7], it can be noted that summaries with images assist in quicker understanding of the results, thereby helping in arriving at relevant judgments faster. Therefore, we define graphic elements as images corresponding to the topic candidates in slides, given that the noun phrases in the surrounding text of the images are similar to the topic candidates. We considered that the images used to describe the content in slides, and a slide title can be a subject of the content. This is calculated using the Simpson similarity coefficient [14]. The surrounding text can be selected from any portion of the slide, from its title to its body (i.e., from the high level to the low level). When the similarity exceeds a predefined threshold, the noun phrases in the surrounding text and the topic candidates are considered similar. Then, the images are recognized as the corresponding images of the topic candidates.

3.2 Determination of Semantic Relationships between Elements

Semantic relationships between elements are determined from a document tree of a presentation to enable users obtain relevant information between the key elements at a glance, for a quick understanding of the content.

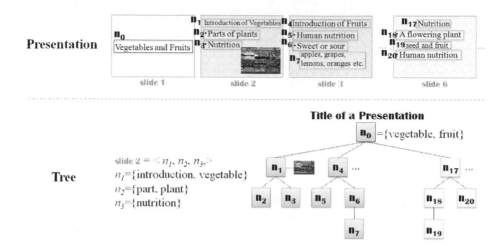

Fig. 3. An example of a presentation and its tree representation

Basic Definitions and Algebra. The presentation shown in Fig. 3 is represented as a rooted ordered tree $D = (N, E)$ with a set of nodes N and a set of edges $E \subseteq N \times N$. There exists a distinguished root node from which the rest of the nodes can be reached by traversing the edges in E. Each node, except the root, has a unique parent node. Each node n of the document tree is associated with a logical component, such as $< title >$ or $< sections >$, based on the bullet points of slides using an XML file in the given presentation. There is a function $words(n)$ that returns the representative noun phrases of the corresponding component in n. A partial tree of the document tree D with a given noun phrase as its root is defined as a fragment f. It can be denoted as $f \subseteq D$. A slide is a fragment by the slide title. In Fig. 3, $< n_1, n_2, n_3 >$ is the set of nodes in slide 2 and a fragment of the sample document tree.

To formally define the semantic relationships between the noun phrases from the extracted elements, we first define operations on fragments, and sets of fragments using a pairwise fragment join [13]. Let F_x and F_y be two sets of fragments in a document tree D of a given presentation, then, the pairwise fragment join of F_x and F_y, denoted as $F_x \bowtie F_y$, is defined to extract a set of fragments. This set is yielded by computing the fragment join of every combination of an element in F_x and an element in F_y, in pairs, as follows:

$$F_x \bowtie F_y = \{f_x \bowtie f_y \mid f_x \in F_x, f_y \in F_y\} \tag{3}$$

Fig. 4 illustrates an example of operation for pairwise fragment join. It refers the sample document tree in Fig. 3. For the given two noun phrase $x = nutrition$ and $y = fruit$, where $F_x = \{< n_3 >, < n_5 >, < n_{17}, n_{18}, n_{19}, n_{20} >, < n_{20} >\}$, $F_y = \{< n_4, n_5, n_6, n_7 >, < n_{19} >\}$, $F_x \bowtie F_y$ produces a set of fragments $\{< n_3 > \bowtie < n_4, n_5, n_6, n_7 >, < n_5 > \bowtie < n_4, n_5, n_6, n_7 >, < n_{17}, n_{18}, n_{19}, n_{20} > \bowtie <$

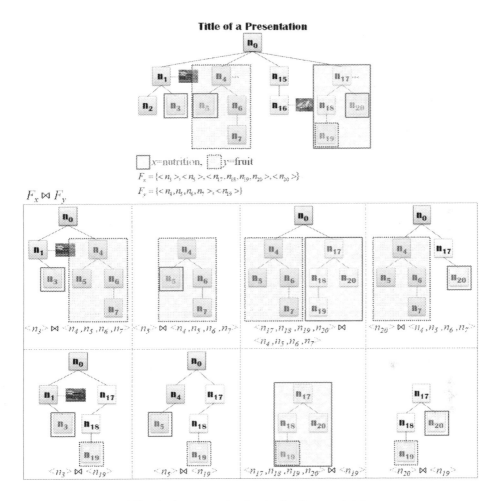

Fig. 4. An example of pairwise fragment join

$n_4, n_5, n_6, n_7 >, < n_{20} >\bowtie< n_4, n_5, n_6, n_7 >, < n_3 >\bowtie< n_{19} >, < n_5 >\bowtie< n_{19} >, < n_{17}, n_{18}, n_{19}, n_{20} >\bowtie< n_{19} >, < n_{20} >\bowtie< n_{19} >\}$ on applying Eq. (3).

Semantic Filters. We determine semantic relationships between the given noun phrases, x and y, from the extracted elements using the set of fragments produced by taking pairwise fragment join as semantic filters. For this, we define four types of semantic filters by considering the horizontal and vertical relevance, as well as the structural semantics from the document tree of the given presentation.

Horizontal Distance. Logically interrelated slides of a presentation are typically close to each other. Therefore, is such presentations, the horizontal distance between nodes in different slides of a document tree is a reasonable measure of the inter-relationship between nodes. Specifically, when the horizontal distance between the nodes in slides containing x and y exceeds a certain threshold, x is irrelevant to y. Supposing, $hdist(t_i, t_j)$ denotes the distance between the nodes of the slide titles t_i and t_j in slides containing x and y, we set the threshold value α at $|N|/2$, i.e., half the total number of nodes N in the document tree, for normalizing various presentations. If $hdist(t_i, t_j)$ does not exceed α, then the distance between two slides containing x and y is short (i.e., relevant); contrarily, if $hdist(t_i, t_j)$ exceeds α, the distance between two slides containing x and y is long (i.e., irrelevant).

Vertical Distance. Logically, indentations of slides are typically close to each other. Therefore, when the distance between the slides containing x and y is long, and x and y are at the low levels in slides, they can be less relevant in the document tree. When vertical distance between the nodes in slides containing x and y exceeds a certain threshold, and x and y are at the low level in the slides, x is irrelevant to y. Supposing, $vdist(r, q)$ denotes the distance between the root node r and the node containing each given noun phrase q (e.g., x or y), we set the threshold value β at $ave(depth)$, which is an average of the depth of levels in the document tree, for normalizing various presentations. If $vdist(r, q)$ does not exceed β, then the level of the node containing x or y is high (i.e., relevant); contrarily, if $vdist(r, q)$ exceeds β, the level of the node containing x or y is low (i.e., irrelevant).

Hierarchy. For judging the semantics of x and y, we compare the levels of x and y in the fragments based on the theory of hierarchical semantics. When $l(x) < l(y)$, it denotes that the level of x is higher than the level of y; x is a superordinate concept of y (y is a subordinate concept of x). Contrarily, $l(x) > l(y)$ denotes that the level of x is lower than the level of y; x is a subordinate concept of y (y is a superordinate concept of x). When $l(x) = l(y)$, this denotes that the level of x is same as the level of y; they have coordinate concept with each other.

Inclusion. We can consider the inclusion relationships between the fragments of x and y. When $f_x \subseteq f_y$, it denotes that the fragment of x is included in the fragment of y, i.e., f_x is a partial tree of f_y. Contrarily, when $f_x \supseteq f_y$, it denotes that the fragment of x includes the fragment of y, i.e., f_y is a partial tree of f_x.

Semantic Relationship Types. We determine five types of semantic relationships between the given noun phrases, x and y, by combining the semantic filters of Table 1. For measuring the relevance between x and y, we focus on the *horizontal distance* and the *vertical distance*. Here, when the *horizontal distance* between them is long, the *vertical distance* should be short. We determine hierarchical relationships, x *shows* y, x *describes* y, and x *likewise* y, by focusing on *hierarchy*. In x *shows* y, $l(x) < l(y)$ means x is a superordinate concept of y (y is a subordinate concept of x). In x *describes* y, $l(x) > l(y)$ means x is a subordinate concept of y (y is a superordinate concept of x). Then, *show* and *describe* are functionally interchangeable, when x *describes* y

Table 1. Semantic relationships with semantic filters

Relationship types	Horizontal distance	Vertical distance	Hierarchy	Inclusion
x shows y	$< \alpha$	*either*	$l(x) < l(y)$	*either*
x shows y	$\geq \alpha$	$< \beta$	$l(x) < l(y)$	*either*
x describes y	$< \alpha$	*either*	$l(x) > l(y)$	*either*
x describes y	$\geq \alpha$	$< \beta$	$l(x) > l(y)$	*either*
x likewise y	$< \alpha$	*either*	$l(x) = l(y)$	*either*
x likewise y	$\geq \alpha$	$< \beta$	$l(x) = l(y)$	*either*
x part-of y	$< \alpha$	*either*	*either*	$f_x \subseteq f_y$
x part-of y	$\geq \alpha$	$< \beta$	*either*	$f_x \subseteq f_y$
x has-a y	$< \alpha$	*either*	*either*	$f_x \supseteq f_y$
x has-a y	$\geq \alpha$	$< \beta$	*either*	$f_x \supseteq f_y$

is from the viewpoint of *y shows x*. In *x likewise y*, $l(x) = l(y)$ means x and y have coordinate concept with each other. We determine inclusion relationships, which are *x part-of y* and *x has-a y*, by focusing on *inclusion*. In *x part-of y*, $f_x \subseteq f_y$ means that the concept of x is included in the concept of y. In *x has-a y*, $f_x \supseteq f_y$ means that the concept of x includes the concept of y. Then, *part-of* and *has-a* are functionally interchangeable, when *x has-a y* is from the viewpoint of *y part-of x*. When x and y fail to match these determinations of semantic relationships, x and y are independent. Therefore, a numbers of semantic relationships between x and y are formed from a set of fragments produced by taking the pairwise fragment join; a semantic relationship is determined by majority.

In this work, the semantic relationships follow a transitivity law, e.g., iff x *shows* y, y *shows* z, then it is assumed that x *shows* z.

4 iPoster: Interactive Poster Generation

We generate an iPoster possessing the following two features: (1) Providing an overview of elements from the slides, retaining this feature of traditional posters; and (2) Utilizing a zooming user interface, reflecting the semantics of the elements and promoting user interaction.

4.1 Determination of Element Layouts

For providing an overview of elements from slides, we attempt to determine the element layouts by utilizing a tree structure combined with a stacked Venn, based on the semantic relationships between the elements. When hierarchical relationships exist between two elements, i.e., either *show*, *describe*, or *likewise* exists between the elements, they reveal a hierarchy between those elements, as applied to a tree structure. *Show* or *describe* maps a parent-child relationship in the tree structure; for instance, if x *shows* y (y *describes* x), then we mark x in a parent area and y in a child area, suggesting that the layer of x is higher than the layer of y. Additionally, *likewise* maps a sibling relationship in the tree structure; for instance, if x *likewise* y, then we locate x and y in the same layer. Inclusion relationships between two elements, i.e., *part-of* and *has-a*, reveals a logical relationship of inclusion and exclusion applied, as to a stacked Venn. For instance, x *part-of* y (y *has-a* x), we conceive an area of x that is included in an area of y, and that the area of y is larger than the area of x.

4.2   Determination of Transitions between Elements

To utilize a zooming user interface for navigating through presentations, the transitions discussed here explain the kinds of visual effects that are applied to the semantic relationship types, to reflect the meaning of the elements from the slides. We animate the zooming and panning transitions for navigating through elements in the structural layout based on the semantic relationship types; this can help users to visually understand the overview and details of the contents within a presentation.

Transitions for *show* (*describe*). When the hierarchical relationship, *show* (*describe*), between two elements is not included in an inclusion relationship, i.e., *part-of* (*has-a*), then, firstly the view must be zoomed-out from the focused element to an overview of the tree structure, following which, it must be zoomed-in to the target element. In addition, when *show* (*descibe*) between two elements is included in the inclusion relationship, the transitions between two elements includes zooming-out from the focused element to the whole element area in the stacked Venn, and zooming-in to the target element. Therefore, the transitions include passing through the overview or the whole element area, which helps users to easily grasp the super-sub relation existing between them.

Transitions for *likewise*. When the hierarchical relationship, *likewise*, exists between two elements, the transitions between the two elements include zooming-out from the focused element to an area enclosing both the elements and their parent element, and then zooming-in to the target element. Therefore, the transitions indicate the presence of the parent element; thereby elucidating to the user the existence of a subservient relationship.

Transitions for *part-of* (*has-a*). When the inclusion relationship, *part-of* (*has-a*), exists between two elements, the transition between the two elements pans from the focused element to the target element. Therefore, this simple and direct transition between the two elements helps users to easily understand that they are dependent on each other, and that there exists an inclusion relationship between them.

In addition to the above, the transitions between two independent elements include zooming-out from the focused element to all elements, and then zooming-in to the target element. Therefore, these transitions help the users to easily know that they are irrelevant with respect to each other in an iPoster.

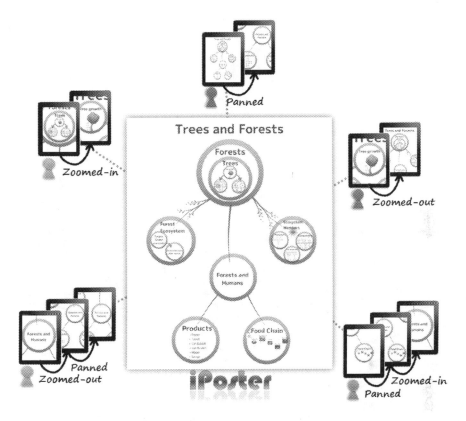

Fig. 5. An example of a collaborative browsing platform based on iPoster

5 Collaborative Browsing Platform Based on iPoster

Based on the method described above, we build a novel collaborative browsing platform that aids users to interactively gain a broad understanding of the presentation slides, based on the usersf operations and our semantic structure analysis. We generated an interactive poster using an online lecture material called "Trees and Forests."[6] As depicted in Fig. 5, our iPoster provides an overview of "Trees and Forests," containing key points such as "Forests," "Forest Ecosystem," "Forests and Humans," "Ecosystem Members," "Products," and "Food Chain." Users A, B, C, D, and E are interactively browsing our iPoster that is shared in the cyberspace, operating on their tablets from anywhere.

In this case of collaborative browsing with iPoster, 1) iPoster can share the most important topics with each other and represent information that meets each user's specific requirements on certain topics, 2) Users can detect other users who have the similar requirements on certain topics and share their interests

---

[6] http://teacherweb.com/AB/GilbertPatersonMiddleSchool/MsDavid/
Tree-Types-2b-Posting-version.ppt

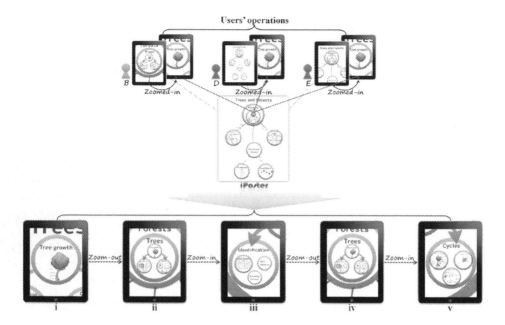

Fig. 6. An example of showing details of 'Tree growth' based on zooming transitions

with each other through their tablets. An example is shown in Fig. 6, the area of "Tree growth" is highlighted on iPoster sharing on all tablets, because of the area of "Tree growth" is zoomed-in on the tablets of B, D, and E by their zoom-in operation. Because "Identification" and "Cycles" *describes* "Tree growth," and are included in "Trees," we assumed that the users want to get details of "Tree growth" with their zoom-in operation. Therefore, the iPoster represents the transitions between the area of "Tree growth" and the areas of its details (including "Identification" and "Cycles") on the tablets of B, D, and E. As shown in Fig. 6, on the tablets of B, D, and E, the iPoster firstly zooms-out from the area of "Tree growth" as shown in **i**, to the whole area of "Trees" as shown in **ii**; this conveys to B, D, and E about the whole concept "Trees," which contains "Tree growth," after that, the iPoster zooms-in to the area of "Identification" as shown in **iii**. This enables B, D, and E to understand that "Identification" is a detail of "Tree growth." Next, the iPoster zooms-out from the area of "Identification" as shown in **iii** to the whole area of "Trees" again as shown in **iv**, following which it zooms-in to the area of "Cycles" as shown in **v**. This enables B, D, and E to comprehend that "Cycles" is a detail of "Tree growth" as well. In general, "Tree growth" is a rather uncommon subject for content; however, in this work, we supposed that it was a topic which is worthy to know, considering that many users focused on it. In addition, we can represent the relevant information based on semantic structure analysis, by deriving the users' requirements from their operations.

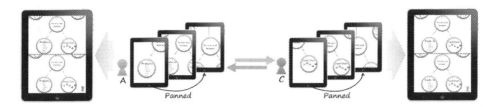

Fig. 7. An example of sharing screens of A and C with each other

On the other hand, when A pans from the area of "Products" to the area of "Forests and Humans," and C pans from the area of "Food Chain" to the area of "Forests and Humans," areas including "Forests and Humans," "Products," and "Food Chain" are represented on their tablets and they can share their screens with each other using their tablets (see Fig. 7). In this case, since "Products" *describes* "Forests and Humans," "Food Chain" *describes* "Forests and Humans," and "Products" *likewise* "Food Chain," based on our semantic structure analysis, we considered that A and C have similar needs concerning the topic "Forests and Humans" by panning from its coordinate subtopics, "Products" and "Food Chain." Then, we display the whole area of "Forests and Humans" and share their screens with each other in order to support them to compare their interests, and to promote their communication.

6   Conclusions and Future Work

In this paper, we built a collaborative browsing platform for presentation slides based on interactive poster generation, called the "iPoster," for presenting elements (i.e., textual and graphic elements) in a meaningfully structured layout with automatic transitions, such as zooms and pans, to promote user interaction. Especially, we introduced a semantic structure analysis model for extracting elements and determining the semantic relationships between the elements of the slides. In order to generate an iPoster in a zoomable canvas, we initially placed the elements in a tree structure combined with a stacked Venn. We then attached the zooming and panning transitions between the elements, based on the semantic relationship types. iPoster enables users to interactively and collaboratively browse, and understand educational presentations easily and efficiently using their tablets.

In the future, we plan to varied structural layouts for generating iPosters to help users intuitively understand traditional presentations. Additionally, we have to confirm that our collaborative browsing method enables users to browse and understand the presentations, meeting their needs effectively and easily. Further, we need to consider the semantic structure analysis on slides by comparing users' operations on an iPoster. We must combine the meanings of the content with the meanings of the users' operation. For instance, if the user zoomed-in from x on y on the iPoster, we can deduce that the user wanted the details of y. However,

x *describes* y and z *describes* y shows that both x and z have the details of y in the slides. Then, we can suggest y zooms-in z to the user, which indicates that z has the details of y that can satisfy the user's requirement.

References

1. Bederson, B.B., Hollan, J.D.: Pad++: a zooming graphical interface for exploring alternate interface physics. In: Proc. of the 7th ACM Symposium on User Interface Software and Technology (UIST 1994), pp. 17–26 (1994)
2. Bouamrane, M., Luz, S.: Meeting Browsing: State-of-the-art-review. In: Multimedia Systems, vol. 12, pp. 439–457 (2007)
3. Good, L., Bederson, B.B.: Zoomable User Interfaces as A Medium for Slide Show Presentations. Journal of Information Visualization 1, 35–49 (2002)
4. Katayama, S., Goda, T., Shiramatsu, S., Ozono, T., Shintani, T.: Implementing a Collaborative Document Revision System with Web Technology (in Japanese). In: Proc. of the 27th Annual Conference of the Japanese Society for Artificial Intelligence (JSAI 2013), vol. 27 (2013)
5. Lanir, J., Booth, R., Tang, A.: MultiPresenter: A Presentation System for (Very) Large Display Surfaces. In: Proc. of the 16th ACM International Conference on Multimedia (MM 2008), pp. 519–528 (2008)
6. Laufer, L., Halacsy, P., Fischer, A.: Prezi Meeting: Collaboration in a Zoomable Canvas Based Environment. In: Proc. of CHI 2011 Extended Abstracts on Human Factors in Computing Systems (CHI EA 2011), pp. 749–752 (2011)
7. Li, Z., Shi, S., Zhang, L.: Improving relevance judgment of web search results with image excerpts. In: Proc. of the 17th International World Wide Web Conference (WWW 2008), pp. 21–30 (2008)
8. Lichtschlag, L., Hess, T., Karrer, T., Borchers, J.: Canvas presentation in the wild. In: Proc. of CHI 2012 Extended Abstracts on Human Factors in Computing Systems (CHI EA 2012), pp. 537–540 (2012)
9. Lichtschlag, L., Karrer, T., Borchers, J.: Fly: A Tool to Author Planar Presentations. In: Proc. of the 27th International Conference on Human Factors in Computing Systems (CHI 2009), pp. 547–556 (2009)
10. Maekawa, T., Uemukai, T., Hara, T., Nishio, S.: Content Description and Partitioning Methods for Collaborative Browsing by Multiple Mobile Users. In: Proc. of the 16th International Workshop on Database and Expert Systems Applications, pp. 1068–1072 (2005)
11. McCloud, S.: Reinventing Comics: How Imagination and Technology Are Revolutionizing an Art Form. Harper (2000)
12. Novak, J., Canas, A.: The Theory Underlying Concept Maps and How To Construct and Use Them. Institute for Human and Machine Cognition, IHMC (2008)
13. Pradhan, S.: An algebraic query model for effective and efficient retrieval of xml fragments. In: Proc. of the 32nd International Conference on Very Large Data Bases (VLDB 2006), pp. 295–306 (2006)
14. Simpson, E.H.: Measurement of Diversity. Nature 163, 688 (1949)
15. Spicer, R., Lin, Y., Lelliher, A., Sundaram, H.: NextSlidePlease: Authoring and Delivering Agile Multimedia Presentations. ACM Transactions on Multimedia Computing, Communication and Applications 8, 53:1–53:20 (2012)
16. Tufte, E.: The cognitive style of powerpoint. Graphics Press, Cheshire (2003)

Using E-mail Communication Network for Importance Measurement in Collaboration Environments

Paweł Lubarski and Mikołaj Morzy

Institute of Computing Science
Poznan University of Technology
Piotrowo 2, 60-965 Poznan, Poland
Pawel.Lubarski@cs.put.poznan.pl, Mikolaj.Morzy@put.poznan.pl

Abstract. Can we establish the importance of people by simply analyzing the set of sent and received emails, having no access to subject lines or contents of messages? The answer, apparently, is "yes we can". Intrinsic behavior of people reveals simple patterns in choosing which emails to answer next. Our theory is based on two assumptions. We assume that people do their email communication in bursts, answering several messages consecutively and that they can freely choose the order of answers. Secondly, we believe that people use priority queues to manage their internal task lists, including the list of emails to be answered. Looking at timing and ordering of responses we derive individual rankings of importance of actors, because we posit that people have a tendency to reply to important actors first. These individual subjective rankings are significant because they reflect the relative importance of other actors as perceived by each actor. The individual rankings are aggregated into a global ranking of importance of all actors. We perform an experimental evaluation of our model by analyzing the dataset consisting of over 600 000 emails sent during one year period to 200 employees of our university. Our final ranking closely reflects the "true" importance of employees computed based on surveys. We think that our model is general and can be applied whenever behavioral data is available which includes any choice made by actors from a set of available alternatives with the alternatives having varying degrees of importance to individual actors.

1 Introduction

Are we all predictable, or are our actions erratic and random by nature? Are there mechanisms that govern our behavior, of which we are not aware, yet these mechanisms make our behavior not-so-mysterious? In this paper we focus on a single aspect of human activity, namely on e-mail communication, but the underlying mechanism that we want to examine has consequences that reach much further. The priority queue mechanism that we will be investigating is responsible for securing the transition of the random influx of e-mail messages into an ordered power-law distribution of response times and e-mail queue sizes. In other words,

A. Nadamoto et al. (Eds.): SocInfo 2013 Workshops, LNCS 8359, pp. 43–54, 2014.

we are observing an ordering mechanism that leads from randomness to order and we want to verify whether the real-world data truly support the hypothesis of the priority queue mechanism.

Unfortunately, we have only the data which reflect human behavior. In this particular case we have a large body of e-mail communication between members of a constrained community (faculty members of a university). This data reflect the internal underlying mechanism of communication ordering. Surprisingly, although the arrival of messages is inherently random, we observe a very high degree of order and consistency in the way e-mail messages are being processed and answered. Our working hypothesis is that each person maintains an internal priority queue that is constantly replenished and refreshed as new e-mail messages arrive. Because each person has her own priorities and subjective rankings of importance (of tasks and other people), at the individual level e-mail messages sent from particular people, or e-mail messages concerning particular tasks, can be re-ordered and re-shuffled differently. The second assumption that we make is that the primary criterion on which priority queue is maintained, is the subjective importance assigned to an e-mail by the individual. According to this assumption, people should tend to answer important e-mail messages first and e-mail messages deemed less important should be constantly pushed down the priority queue. As the result, the least important messages may stay at the bottom of the priority queue for a very long time and may never be answered. On the other hand, some e-mail messages will always jump to the top of the priority queue. This simple mechanism by itself may be responsible for power-law distributions of response times that we observe in the data.

We need to clarify an important issue at this point. Although in our model individuals may assign importance both to people and to tasks, we must limit our investigation to the importance of people only. The reason is that due to privacy concerns we did not have access to either the contents or the subject lines of e-mail messages, thus we cannot make any inferences about the semantic context of e-mail communication between faculty members. The identities of both sender and receiver were revealed, so we are able to correlate our results with an objective, outsider view of the importance of each person (as determined by one's academic title and administrative position). Furthermore, the community under investigation is reasonably large (almost 200 hundred employees), yet small enough so that every person knows all other employees either directly, or indirectly, and is able to establish a subjective perception of the importance of every other employee.

Our study has been performed on a constrained community. There is a possibility that there are some latent variables that influence the final outcome. For instance, it could be that since actors are aware of academic titles and positions of other actors, the positions and titles influence the order of email responses. In such case our findings would be much more difficult to apply to open collaboration environments in which it is assumed that actors do not know each other (at least at the beginning of the collaboration). However, as we will see in the experimental evaluation of our model, the results seem to suggest that actors indeed use their subjective individual rankings of importance. We constantly see professors from outside of a given actor's group being ranked lower than actors from within the group. The exact measurement of this phenomenon has not been performed yet and is the subject of our future work.

Our paper is organized as follows. First, we describe previous work related to our research in Section 2. Then, we introduce basic notation used throughout the paper and we formulate the mathematical model of e-mail processing in Section 3. Section 4 describes the dataset used in the experiments and reports on the results of conducted studies. We present the results of an accompanying survey in Section 5. Finally, we conclude the paper in Section 6 with a short summary and a future work agenda.

2 Related Work

E-mail communication analysis has been a popular area of research in the domain of social network analysis in recent years. Most efforts were directed on fighting spam [3,5], deriving the shape of personal social networks based on the contents of one's inbox [6,2], and mining various patterns in e-mail networks [10,11]. An example of the later was the analysis of the communication patterns within the Enron corporation shortly before the outbreak of the scandal [7].

The method presented in this work is grounded in the theory of queueing [9]. Our immediate inspiration comes from the work of Barabási, who has suggested the connection between priority queues and emergent power law distributions [1]. Since we are interested in establishing the subjective importance of actors based on e-mail communication, our method may be perceived through the lens of personalization [14] and ranking. The later has been the subject of much research, in particular in the context of partial aggregation of ranking lists of search engine query results [8].

Finally, our work concerns the analysis of e-mail usage patterns. This issue has been researched for many years on the grounds of behavioral science [13], psychology [4], and sociology [12].

3 Basic Definitions

Let us now proceed to the presentation of the basic analytical model used in our experiments. Let $U = \{u_1, \ldots, u_n\}$ be the set of users. Let m_{ij}^t be an e-mail message sent from the user u_i to the user u_j at the timestamp t, and let M denote the set of all available messages. We are interested in reciprocal communication, thus we will concentrate only on the messages that were replied. If we can find a pair of messages m_{ij}^t and $m_{ji}^{t'}$ such that $t < t' \wedge \not\exists m_{ji}^{t''} : t'' < t'$ then we say that users u_i and u_j have communicated and we denote this fact by $c_{ij}^{t'}$ (note that we use the timestamp of the reply as the marker for communication). Since, as we have previously pointed out, we did not have access to subject lines of e-mail messages or to the "In-Reply-To" header of the SMTP protocol, we were unable to recreate the threads of communication. Thus, we make an additional simplifying assumption that users communicate in a serial mode using first-in-first-out mode. Each communication has the delay $\tau(c_{ij}^t) = |t' - t|$ which reflects the amount of time it took for the user u_j to answer the message. With each user u_i we associate a message queue $Q^{t'}(u_i) = \{m_{ki}^t : t < t' \wedge \nexists c_{ki}^{t'}, u_k, u_i \in U\}$ consisting of all e-mail messages received by the user u_i until time t which have not been yet replied to. The number of messages that have arrived to the user's inbox in-between the delay $\tau(c_{ij}^{t'})$ is called the *delay queue* and we will denote it with $q(c_{ij}^{t'}) = abs(|Q^{t'}(u_i)| - |Q^t(u_i)|)$.

Our goal is to compute the global ranking of users based on the individual subjective rankings of importance as perceived by all individual users. Let $R(u_i)$ denote the final global ranking of the user u_i. Then, $R(u_i) = \sum_{u_k \in U} w_{ki} R(u_k)$ where w_{ki} is the weight of communication between users u_k and u_i. We think of w_{ki} as the measure of subjective importance, i.e., w_{ki} reflects how important is the user u_i in the eyes of the user u_k. If there were several instances of communication between users u_k and u_i, we average the final weight over all communications between this pair of users. But how do we arrive at a particular weight of communication between users? There are many ways in which we may use the available data to compute this weight. Below we present three exemplary weighting schemes, but it is worth noting that our model should work independently of the particular weighting scheme.

3.1   Delay Factor

The first weighting scheme assumes that people usually work in daily batches and most people expect their e-mail messages to be answered within a single working day. Therefore, if a message has been answered in less than 8 hours, this signifies that there was no unnecessary delay, and thus we may conclude that the sender of the message was perceived by the receiver of the message as an important person. Formally, the weight of the communication is defined as:

$$w_{ij}^{DF} = \begin{cases} 1 & \text{if } \tau(c_{ij}^t) < 8 \\ \frac{1}{\tau(c_{ij}^t) - 8} & \text{otherwise} \end{cases} \tag{1}$$

3.2   Queue Number

In this weighting scheme we define the e-mail message to be important if it was succeeded by a long queue of unanswered messages. In other words, the importance of the message (and, by extension, of the sender of the message) is defined by the number of messages that the given message has preceded. Since user queues can be arbitrarily long and without normalization we would assign a far too large weight to messages answered by people who generally tend to have long queues of unanswered e-mail messages, we have decided to introduce an arbitrary limit of the e-mail message queue and set it to 15. Of course, changing this parameter only introduces a linear scaling of the weight without disrupting of relative weights between pairs of users. Mathematically we define the queue number weight as:

$$w_{ij}^{QN} = \begin{cases} 15 - q(c_{ij}^t) & \text{if } q(c_{ij}^t) <= 15 \\ 0 & \text{if } q(c_{ij}^t) > 15 \end{cases} \tag{2}$$

3.3   Queue Factor

The final weighting scheme aims at identifying e-mail messages that tend to interrupt the regular processing of the message queue. This is to say that the weight of the message is proportional to the number of older e-mail messages that have been shifted down the priority queue by the arrival of the message. Accordingly to this scheme, if a message arrives at the inbox of the user u_i and the user decides to answer it immediately (such message shifts all other messages down by one position in the queue), this indicates that the sender of the message is very important to the receiver. On the other hand, if the new message is filed by the receiver somewhere in the priority queue and answered at some later point in time, this may be interpreted as the indication that the sender of the message is not perceived as important. Formally, the scheme is defined as:

$$w_{ij}^{QF} = \frac{\left|Q_{u_i}^t\right| - q(c_{ij}^t)}{\left|Q_{u_i}^t\right|} \tag{3}$$

For the above weighting schemes we compute the global rankings of users by the following procedure. First, we create a graph in which users are represented by vertices and communications are represented by valued edges, with the weight of the communication used as the value of the edge. Next, we compute the eigenvector centrality of vertices. In order to verify the correctness of our weighting schemes we compare the results to the eigenvector centrality computed from a simple graph, where all edges have equal value of 1 irrespective of their weights. In the text section we will describe the experimental protocol and the computed rankings.

4   Experiments

The dataset used in our experiments contains the one year of e-mail communication within the Institute of Computing Science at Poznan University of Technology. The dataset consists of 637 284 e-mail messages exchanged between 126 224 users, of which 188 users were faculty members of the Institute (all the remaining users are either senders or recipients of e-mail messages). Prior to experiments the dataset has been sanitized by removing automatically generated messages, removing messages marked as spam, removing messages with an empty sender header, and aggregating user accounts referring to the same physical person (faculty members can use different aliases for their e-mail addresses). Below we present the distributions of sent and received messages, as well as the distribution of message queue lengths. From Figure 1 we can clearly see that the data is

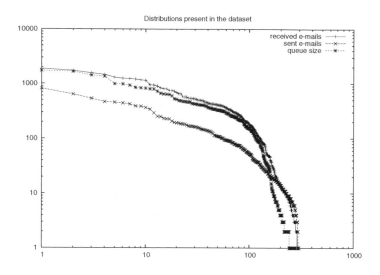

Fig. 1. Data distributions

distributed accordingly to the power-law distribution with an exponential cut-off as defined by $P(k) = k^{-\alpha}e^{k\beta}$.

A difficult question arises of how to verify whether the ranking obtained by the eigenvector centrality measure on e-mail communication graph is correct, i.e. whether it closely represents the "true" importance of users. We have decided to use the following validation protocol: we have manually compiled the list of all employees of the Institute with their respective positions within the organization. These positions represent either academic titles held by the employees (PhD students, associate professors, tenured professors) or their administrative responsibilities (vice-dean, head of the EU research project, etc.). Each position has been awarded a certain amount of points that reflect the objective importance of the position (irrespective of the person holding the position). For instance, tenured professors were awarded 80 points while PhD students were awarded 10 points. The particular choice of points is indeed arbitrary, but our goal was to create a relative ordering of all positions. For a given final ranking of employees we have divided the list of employees into 10-element bins and we have aggregated points in each bin. The rationale behind this step is that the moving sum should be monotonically decreasing if the ranking is close to the objective ranking. In other words, the ranking should not place many "low-point" employees above "high-point" employees if the monotonicity is to be maintained. We present the results of three exemplary rankings in Figure 2.

What we can see is that although rankings are generally monotonically decreasing, there are some sudden jumps in aggregate point sums within consecutive buckets. Each such increase suggests, that the ranking placed a group of "low-point" employees (e.g. assistant professors) above "high-point" employees (e.g. tenured professors). By itself it needs not to be an error, because there can

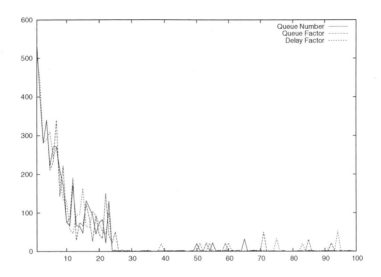

Fig. 2. Moving sums of rankings

be certain employees who are regarded highly by the community despite their relative low scientific and administrative positions, but in general such situation should concern only a few employees (and therefore should not impact the sum of points of a 10 element bucket). After carefully scrutinizing the data we have found that quite often e-mail communication of users has been interrupted by relatively unimportant messages that were nevertheless answered very quickly. In particular, this applies to messages for which the effort of answer is very low (for instance, when the answer consisted of a single word or a sentence).

Thus we have modified our model to control for such e-mail messages. For each message we compute the effort required to prepare the message, using the time between sending of consecutive e-mail messages as a proxy for effort. Then, we discard all e-mail messages that were effortless to prepare (e.g., we remove e-mail messages prepared within less than 30 seconds). The rationale behind this procedure is that people tend to put much more effort in writing e-mail messages addressed to people whom they deem important (which includes grammatical correctness, checking for punctuation, stylistic refinement of text, etc.). After this modification our final global rankings become monotonically decreasing, as presented in Figure 3, where reference is the moving sum of rankings without considering effort, while additive and identity effort are two weighting schemes in which either the weight is increased by the effort (additive) or replaced by the effort (identity).

In order to further verify the correctness of the approach we checked if there were any significant differences in rankings produced by various weighting schemes (schemes using user weighting are denoted with a letter "w"). Table 1 presents the correlations between rankings (both Spearman's footrule distance and Kendall's τ distance produced identical results up to two digits of precision). We note that

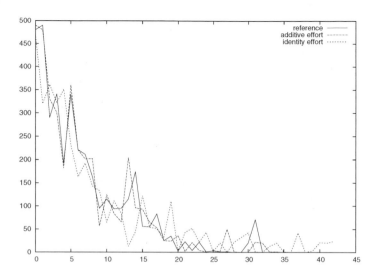

Fig. 3. Moving sums of rankings when effort is considered

Table 1. Similarity between rankings shown by Spearman's ρ and Kendall's τ

	DF	DF(w)	QN	QN(w)	QF	QF(w)
DF	1,00	0,85	1,00	0,87	0,85	0,85
DF(w)	0,85	1,00	0,85	0,88	0,90	0,90
QN	1,00	0,85	1,00	0,87	0,85	0,85
QN(w)	0,87	0,88	0,87	1,00	0,88	0,88
QF	0,85	0,90	0,85	0,88	1,00	0,90
QF(w)	0,85	0,90	0,85	0,88	0,90	1,00

the weighting schemes produce surprisingly consistent results, which allows us to conclude that the underlying model of priority queues is correct.

5   Survey

In order to further verify the correctness of our approach we have run a survey among the employees of the Institute. The survey has been answered by 73 employees aged 24 to 65, with mean age of slightly under 33 years ($\mu = 32.8$, $\sigma = 1.25$), women ($n = 15$) are slightly younger ($\mu = 30$, $\sigma = 1.14$) but the difference is not statistically significant ($z = 0.049$, $p = 0.961$). Most surveyed employees were PhD students (68.5%), with some associate professors (26%) and tenured professors (4.1%). Administrative positions were held by 12 employees (16.4%), and 10 employees were in charge of a research project (13.7%). The aim of the survey was to establish the most popular strategies of processing of the incoming e-mail messages and to discover which delays the employees were willing to impose on the incoming e-mails consciously. Table 2 shows the

Table 2. Correlation between the order of answers and the duration of the delay

	sample size	correlation	significance
friends	73	0.287	0.014
co-workers	73	0.197	0.095
supervisors	73	0.282	0.016
administration	73	0.273	0.020
students	73	0.223	0.058
M.Sc. students	73	0.212	0.072

tendency to procrastinate and the preferred order of answering e-mail messages conditioned on the type of the sender expressed using five-point Likert scale.

In the first order employees tend to answer to their supervisors and co-workers, but e-mails from supervisors tend to be answered quicker. Students and M.Sc. students have to wait the longest, and friends are answered slightly faster than the administration. The correlations between the two variables are not large, but except for the situation in which the sender is a co-worker or a M.Sc. student, there is a positive relationship between the order of answering and the duration of the delay. Table below presents the correlation coefficients and the levels of statistical significance.

Table 3. Descriptive statistics for e-mail processing strategies

strategy	homogeneous groups by Friedman test ($p < 0.05$)	μ	σ
S5	First I answer e-mails concerning important issues	8.81	1.578
S7	Sender is important when deciding the order of answers	7.95	2.185
S1	I try to read all new e-mails in my inbox	7.32	2.350
S10	E-mail processing is the first task I do at the beginning of a day	6.53	2.450
S11	First thing I do is to remove junk and spam e-mail	6.45	2.872
S4	During a single session I answer only a part of my e-mail	6.32	2.560
S2	Usually I answer a part of my e-mail and switch to other tasks	6.16	2.404
S8	I pay more attention to the sender than to the subject	5.92	2.564
S3	I try to answer all e-mails before switching to other tasks	4.62	2.301
S6	I prefer to answer e-mails in the order of their arrivals	4.42	2.582
S9	I sort new e-mails into groups and folders based on their important	3.82	2.997

The main variable in the survey is the strategy of e-mail message communication processing. Based on previous research we have identified 11 primary strategies outlined in Table 3. The most popular strategies are S5 (answering important e-mails first) and S7 (prioritizing e-mails from important senders), while the least popular strategies are S6 (answering e-mail messages in the order of arrival) and S9 (sorting e-mails using folders and labels).

Table 4. Correlations between e-mail processing strategies

	S1	S2	S3	S4	S5	S6	S7	S8	S9	S10
S2	-0.163									
S3	0.340	-0.436								
S4	-0.318	0.518	-0.559							
S5	0.083	0.082	0.064	0.062						
S6	0.194	-0.029	0.151	0.040	-0.060					
S7	-0.031	0.152	-0.145	0.038	0.177	0.085				
S8	-0.121	0.178	-0.017	-0.028	-0.064	-0.045	0.465			
S9	-0.076	0.037	0.026	-0.106	0.130	0.020	0.275	-0.025		
S10	0.260	-0.114	0.106	-0.017	-0.042	0.183	0.042	0.148	-0.182	
S11	0.263	-0.040	0.072	-0.095	0.028	0.066	0.159	0.042	0.032	0.152

We have not found any significant differences in the preferences for these strategies among types of employees, with the sole exception of the strategy S4 (partial processing of the inbox) preferred by employees with a Ph.D. or higher ($z = 2.24$, $p = 0.025$) and older employees ($\rho = 0.247$, $p = 0.036$). In order to better understand the relationships between strategies we have performed a two-dimensional scaling of strategies, with the results depicted in Figure 4.

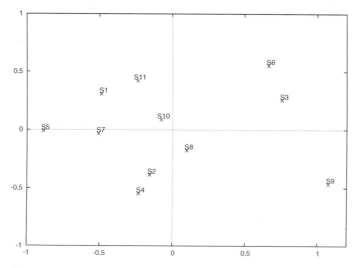

Fig. 4. Two-dimensional scaling of e-mail processing strategies

Some of the strategies were complementary, while others were mutually exclusive. In Table 4 we present the correlations between strategies. We see for instance that the strategy S1 is positively correlated with the strategy S3 (after opening the inbox the employee reads all e-mail messages and tries to answer them all before switching to another task), similarly strategies S7 and S8 are often used together (the sender is important when deciding the order of answers, the employee pays more attention to the sender than to the subject).

6   Conclusions

In this paper we have presented the results of the examination of a large dataset of e-mail messages exchanged between the constrained group of employees of an institution. Our research focused on using the theory of priority queues to derive the subjective perception of importance of actors within the community, by measuring solely the delays in answering e-mail messages. The results of conducted experiments seem to strongly support our hypothesis that the process of managing e-mail communication is indeed governed by the priority queue mechanism implicitly influencing the behavior of users. Our findings are preliminary and in the near future we want to further investigate this mechanism. In particular, we want to verify the priority queue model in other environments where the act of implicit ordering of actions may not be as pronounced as with e-mail message answering. The ultimate goal is to establish whether a broad range of human activity in which we observe the transition from randomness to order (as attained by the emergence of power law distributions) can be attributed to the general priority queue mechanism. Although our experiments have been conducted on a constrained community of actors who have (more or less) the knowledge of the global state of importance, we are tempted to argue that the findings are more general and apply equally to open collaboration environments. The main reason for this conclusion is the fact that preliminary experiments strongly suggest that it is indeed the priority queue mechanism that governs the behavior of humans when using e-mail communication. If this is so, there should be no reason for the model not to work in open collaboration environments, in which the global state of importance is not known to all actors.

References

1. Barabasi, A.-L.: The origin of bursts and heavy tails in human dynamics. Nature 435(7039), 207–211 (2005)
2. Bird, C., Gourley, A., Devanbu, P., Gertz, M., Swaminathan, A.: Mining email social networks. In: Proceedings of the 2006 International Workshop on Mining Software Repositories, pp. 137–143. ACM (2006)
3. Blanzieri, E., Bryl, A.: A survey of learning-based techniques of email spam filtering. Artificial Intelligence Review 29(1), 63–92 (2008)
4. Burton-Jones, A., Hubona, G.S.: Individual differences and usage behavior: revisiting a technology acceptance model assumption. ACM SIGMIS Database 36(2), 58–77 (2005)
5. Cormack, G.V.: Email spam filtering: A systematic review. Foundations and Trends in Information Retrieval 1(4), 335–455 (2007)
6. Culotta, A., Bekkerman, R., McCallum, A.: Extracting social networks and contact information from email and the web (2004)
7. Diesner, J., Carley, K.M.: Exploration of communication networks from the enron email corpus. In: SIAM Int. Conference on Data Mining: Workshop on Link Analysis, Counterterrorism and Security, Newport Beach, CA. Citeseer (2005)
8. Dwork, C., Kumar, R., Naor, M., Sivakumar, D.: Rank aggregation methods for the web. In: Proc. of the 10th International Conference on World Wide Web, pp. 613–622. ACM (2001)

9. Gross, D., Shortle, J.F., Thompson, J.M., Harris, C.M.: Fundamentals of queueing theory. Wiley.com (2013)
10. Li, H., Zhang, J., Wang, H., Huang, S.: A mining algorithm for email's relationships based on neural networks. In: 2008 International Conference on Computer Science and Software Engineering, vol. 4, pp. 1122–1125. IEEE (2008)
11. Lubarski, P., Morzy, M.: Measuring the importance of users in a social network based on email communication patterns. In: Proceedings of the 2012 International Conference on Advances in Social Networks Analysis and Mining (ASONAM 2012), pp. 86–90. IEEE Computer Society (2012)
12. Whittaker, S., Bellotti, V., Gwizdka, J.: Email in personal information management. Communications of the ACM 49(1), 68–73 (2006)
13. Whittaker, S., Sidner, C.: Email overload: exploring personal information management of email. In: Proceedings of the SIGCHI Conference on Human Factors in Computing Systems, pp. 276–283. ACM (1996)
14. Yoo, S., Yang, Y., Lin, F., Moon, I.-C.: Mining social networks for personalized email prioritization. In: Proc. of the 15th ACM SIGKDD Int. Conference on Knowledge Discovery and Data Mining, pp. 967–976. ACM (2009)

Predicting Best Answerers for New Questions: An Approach Leveraging Topic Modeling and Collaborative Voting

Yuan Tian, Pavneet Singh Kochhar, Ee-Peng Lim, Feida Zhu, and David Lo

Singapore Management University, Singapore
{yuan.tian.2012,kochharps.2012,eplim,fdzhu,davidlo}@smu.edu.sg

Abstract. Community Question Answering (CQA) sites are becoming increasingly important source of information where users can share knowledge on various topics. Although these platforms bring new opportunities for users to seek help or provide solutions, they also pose many challenges with the ever growing size of the community. The sheer number of questions posted everyday motivates the problem of routing questions to the appropriate users who can answer them. In this paper, we propose an approach to predict the best answerer for a new question on CQA site. Our approach considers both user interest and user expertise relevant to the topics of the given question. A user's interests on various topics are learned by applying topic modeling to previous questions answered by the user, while the user's expertise is learned by leveraging collaborative voting mechanism of CQA sites. We have applied our model on a dataset extracted from StackOverflow, one of the biggest CQA sites. The results show that our approach outperforms the TF-IDF based approach.

Keywords: CQA, expert recommendation, topic modeling, collaborative voting.

1 Introduction

Community Question Answering (CQA) sites archive millions of questions and answers posted by users. General CQA sites like Yahoo! Answers[1] and Quora[2], and domain-specific CQA sites like StackOverflow[3] and Mathematics[4] have attracted millions of users. CQA sites provide platforms for users to collaborate in the form of asking questions or giving answers. The main purpose of such communities is to provide high quality answers[5] and to offer a wide variety of

---

[1] http://answers.yahoo.com/

[2] https://www.quora.com/

[3] http://stackoverflow.com

[4] math.stackexchange.com

[5] High quality answers are the answers that satisfy question asker [1] and other web users who face similar problem in the future [2].

A. Nadamoto et al. (Eds.): SocInfo 2013 Workshops, LNCS 8359, pp. 55–68, 2014.
© Springer-Verlag Berlin Heidelberg 2014

solutions or explanations. To maintain high quality questions and answers, most of the CQA sites use collaborative voting mechanism, which allows users inside the community to vote up or down the questions and the answers that they like or dislike. These question answering communities act as collaboration networks of millions of users, which continue to generate huge amount of useful web content.

Currently, users of CQA sites post their questions and wait for other users to post answers to the question, which may even take several days. Even if someone posts the answers, the asker is sometimes not satisfied with the quality of the answer. In both the cases, a system that could recommend questions to suitable users is needed. The goal of such system is to link questions with experts who have higher likelihood of answering these questions. Such a system can contribute towards creation of high quality answers for questions and reducing the time of collecting high quality answer.

In this paper, we propose an approach to recommend lists of users, who can give high quality answers to new questions posted on CQA sites. Our main assumptions are: (1) best answerer would have high interest and expertise on the given question, (2) questions are generated from topics, (3) user expertise and interest on questions are affected by user expertise and interest on related topics. Based on the above assumptions, we collect historical answered questions, together with their answers, to generate profiles for each user. We apply the Latent Dirichlet Allocation (LDA) model on the user profiles to learn their interests on various topics. User topical expertise is modeled based on the voting information of historical answered questions. We make use of collaborative voting mechanism because it is supported by most of the CQA sites like Yahoo! Answers, StackOverflow, and etc. In addition, votes of an answer implies the answerer's expertise on related topics. We propose a model to represent the probability of a user to provide high quality answer to a particular question, by considering the user's interests and expertise on the topics of the question. The inputs to our approach are historical answered questions for each user and a new question, while the output is a list of users who are ranked by their probabilities of being the best answerer of the question. We have applied our approach to a corpus of questions and answers from StackOverflow, one of the biggest CQA sites. The results show that our approach outperforms the TF-IDF based approach.

The contributions of our paper are:

- We propose a new method to predict the best answerers for new questions on Community Question Answering (CQA) sites. Our approach considers both user interests and user expertise on topics of questions.
- Our approach learns user topical interest and expertise from historical answered questions, by leveraging topic modeling and collaborative voting mechanism.
- We compare our approach with a TF-IDF based approach on more than 99,000 questions extracted from StackOverflow, one of the biggest CQA sites. Our experiments show that our approach performs better than the TF-IDF based approach.

The structure of this paper is as follows. In Section 2, we describe previous related work. Next, we describe background information about StackOverflow and a baseline approach in Section 3. In Section 4, we introduce our approach for predicting best answerers for new questions. We analyze experiment results in Section 5. We conclude and mention future work in Section 6.

2   Related Work

Recommending the best answerer is a hot topic in the CQA research area and has garnered interest of many researchers. Several studies present algorithms to discover authorities in the communities [3,4]. Liu et al. applied information retrieval (IR) techniques to find experts on CQA site [3]. They computed a textual similarity between users' previously answered questions and new questions, and ranked the users according to the similarities. Zhang et al. leveraged network based algorithms such as PageRank and HITS to study network structure of Java Forum [4]. They proposed a method named ExpertiseRank based on a new authority evaluation metric Z-score and compared it with other network based recommendation methods. Qu et al. analyzed Yahoo! Answers and suggested that CQA sites should recommend questions to users who are interested in them [5]. They applied the Probabilistic Latent Semantic Analysis (PLSA) to model user interest. Liu et al. modeled answerers' behavior on Yahoo! Answers [6]. They investigated when and how answerers select and answer question. Different from above studies, we assume that questions are generated from topics, and we consider both user interest and user expertise on topic layer. We also leverage collaborative voting mechanism at CQA sites.

Our work is closely related to the following two studies. Liu et al. predicted the best answerer for new questions based on a model that combines language model and the Latent Dirichlet Allocation (LDA) Model [7]. They regarded users' reputation and activity as the prior probability of the user to answer a question. We follow their definition of user activity. However, instead of directly using the reputation of user as prior, we computer user expertise for each question. Riahi et al. recommended expert users through user profile collected from all the best answers given by users [8]. They tested different topic models, such as LDA and Segmented Topic Model (STM) on user profiles. However, they did not consider votes of questions and answers, as well as user activity.

3   Preliminary

3.1   StackOverflow

StackOverflow is one of the biggest question answering site where users can share knowledge, seek expert advice on a wide range of topics in computer programming. Users on StackOverflow have the ability to ask and answer questions, to vote questions up and down and several other features. StackOverflow employs gamification techniques to reward users for performing various set of actions.

Rewards include earning reputation points and badges, which when crosses the threshold, gives additional privileges to the users.

With more than 1.7 million users and over 4,000,000 questions, StackOverflow has become a huge knowledge repository. Each question is assigned tags according to the topic which question belongs to. The top six most discussed topics on the site are: C#, Java, PHP, JavaScript, Android and jQuery. Most of the questions are generally related to a specific programming problem, a software algorithm or software tools.

Each user has a reputation score, which signifies how much community trusts that user. Each question and answer can be voted up or down by other users who feel whether that question or answer is useful or not. Each question voted up fetches +5 for the user whereas each answer voted up increases the reputation of the user by 10 points. User loses reputation by 2 when an answer is voted down. Asker can accept one of the answers as the best answer, then the reputation of the best answer provider will increase by 15. Also, there is a limit on the votes that can be casted by a person in a day. Based on reputation points, users are given privileges like edit posts, retag questions, vote to close, reopen, or migrate any questions etc.

3.2   Baseline Approach Based on TF-IDF

Ranking potential answerers based on the similarities between their profiles and new questions is a basic approach to solve the best answerer prediction problem. The underlying idea is that, given a new question, the user who have answered similar questions should be recommended to answer the question. In this approach, user profiles and questions are stored as documents. TF-IDF based Vector Space Model is applied, where each document is represented as a vector of weighted features. Features are the words appearing in the document, and TF-IDF values are computed as the weights of features. Given one user content profile θ_u and a new question q, the approach ranks the users based on the cosine similarity between θ_u and q. The cosine similarity is denoted as

$$s(\theta_u, q) = \frac{\sum_w tfidf(w, \theta u)tfidf(w, q)}{\sqrt{tfidf(w, \theta u)^2}\sqrt{tfidf(w, q)^2}} \qquad (1)$$

where w refers to words that appears in both user u's profile and question q. $tfidf(w, \theta u)$ is the tfidf weight of word w in θ_u. $tfidf(w, q)$ means the TF-IDF weight of word w in question q. Here, the TF-IDF weight of a word w in a given document d is defined as

$$tfidf(w, d) = \frac{f(w, d)}{\max\{f(w, d) : w \in d\}} \log \frac{|D|}{|\{d \in D : t \in d\}|} \qquad (2)$$

where D denotes a collection of documents.

4   Approach

4.1   Overall Framework

In this section, we present the overall framework of our approach. The framework is illustrated in Figure 1. It contains four main parts: data preprocessing, user profile building, user topical interest & expertise learning, and ranking model building. Firstly, we generate user profiles from the previously answered questions. These profiles include both the textual information and voting information, which is then used to learn the topics as well as user interest and expertise on each learned topic. We propose a ranking model to compute the probability that a user becomes the best answerer of a given question. User interest and expertise on topics are captured in the ranking model. Finally, for each question in testing data, we rank the users based on the probability and find the Top-K users who have higher chances to provide the best answer. We introduce the major parts of our approach in details in the following subsections.

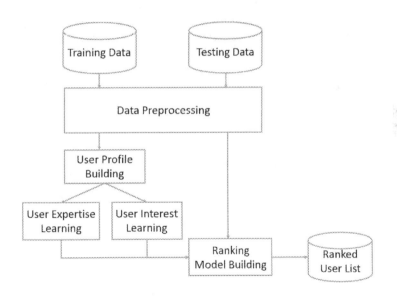

Fig. 1. Overall framework

4.2   Data Preprocessing

We crawl web pages of StackOverflow and collect questions and answers posted during year 2012 under tag "C#", which has the most number of questions among all tags on StackOverflow[6]. Next, we extract both textual and code content for a post (question or answer) from the raw data and then implement the

---

[6] http://stackoverflow.com/tags

general text pre-processing steps: tokenization, stop-word removal, and stemming. Note that the content of a post includes code information, we add some special processes for code content to make the data clean, such as removing keywords in programming language, splitting function name, etc. Cleaned data is then separated into two parts: training dataset and testing dataset. Training data are used to learn user interest and user expertise on topics, while testing data are used to evaluate our approach. For training data, to avoid the impact of bias generated from especially high and low frequency tokens on our ranking model, we rank all the appeared tokens based on the term frequency. By default, tokens ranked in the top 1% and bottom 1% of the ranked list are removed from the corpus. Besides the textual and code information, voting information of answers are also recorded. For a particular answer, the voting information contains: votes and whether this answer has been accepted as the best answer by the asker.

4.3   User Profile Building

Each user profile contains all the answers provided by the user and their corresponding questions. To build these user profiles, we scan all the questions posted during a period of time, and find the users who have answered it. We then put the given answer, together with the question, to the profile of the answerer. In this work, we consider active users on StackOverflow as the potential answerers for new questions, based on the fact that only few of users on StackOverflow are responsible for a large number of questions [9,10]. This means only the profiles of the active users are used as training dataset.

4.4   Ranking Model

To predict the best answerer for a new question, we introduce a probability model. Formally, given a new question q, the probability of a user u being the best answerer for the question is defined as

$$P(u|q) = \frac{P(u)P(q|u)}{P(q)} \tag{3}$$

where $P(u)$ is a prior probability of user u to answer a question, and $P(q|u)$ denotes the probability of generating question q from user u's profile. $P(q)$ refers to a probability related with the question, which remains the same for all potential answerers. Therefore, we can rank answerers just based on the value of $P(u) \times P(q|u)$. Next, we describe the details to calculate $P(u)$ and $P(q|u)$.

Probability of Generating Question from User Profile. Intuitively, user's answering behavior would be affected by his or her interest and expertise on the question. In other words, users who are interested in the question and also have the expertise related to the question are more likely to be the best answerer of the question. Based on this assumption, we compute the value of

$P(q|u)$ from two aspects: user interest and user expertise. The final probability model is computed as

$$P(q|u) = \prod_{w \in q} P(w|\theta_u)^{n(w,q)} \qquad (4)$$

$$P(w|\theta_u) = (1 - \lambda)P_{interest}(w|\theta_u) + \lambda P_{expertise}(w|\theta_u) \qquad (5)$$

Equation 4 is formed based on the assumption that each word in the new question q is generated independently. θ_u presents the profile of user u including both the content profile and the voting profile. $n(w, q)$ is the number of times that word w appears in question q.

Equation 5 states how we compute $P(w|\theta_u)$ by considering both user interest and user expertise. λ is a parameter to control the impact of these two aspects on the value of $P(w|\theta_u)$. In conclusion, our main tasks next are computing $P(u)$, $P_{interest}(w|\theta_u)$, and $P_{expertise}(w|\theta_u)$, respectively.

Prior Information of Answerers. In this work, we model $P(u)$, the prior probability of user u based on the activity of the user. Whenever a user posts a question, he or she wants the answer which is correct as well as timely. Some users could be active for a long time and they continue to give answers to newly posted questions whereas other ones answer occasionally. Therefore, we consider the activity of the user i.e., if a user gave an answer closer to the first question appearing in the test data, that user has a higher activity. In other words, a user who answered questions frequently in the beginning but lately gave very few or no answers would have a lower activity. Based on above assumption, we follow the work of Liu et al. [7] and define the user activity for a given question as

$$P(u) = Activity(u) = exp^{-(t_q - t_u)} \qquad (6)$$

where t_q is the posting time of the new question in test data, t_u is the most recent time when the user authored an answer to a question.

4.5 Modeling User Topical Interest

A user will respond to particular question only if that question is related to the interest area of that user. So, we model user's interest based on the previous responses or answering history of that particular user as it shows the interest of the user on a particular topic. We use all the answers given by a particular user as well as the questions of all these answers to build up the user profile. The user profile has some latent topics within it.

One of the important problems in natural language processing is the lexical gap problem [11]. Language model used in various studies is based only on words matching and does not consider semantic information. So, it does not addresses the problem of lexical gaps between new questions and user profiles. Users have interests on several topics. In a typical context, user tries to choose the topic which he finds most interesting and then narrows down on the questions related to that topic. We use latent dirichlet allocation (LDA) model [12], which has been widely used in information retrieval. LDA has the ability to model topics in large corpus i.e., user profiles in our experiment. LDA model is represented as graphical model.

The topic mixture in LDA is drawn from a conjugate Dirichlet prior, which remains same for all the users. The process of generating user profile θ_u for a specific user u is shown in Figure 2 and described as follows: 1) ϕ_z is the multinomial distribution for each topic z from a Dirichlet distribution with parameter β. ϕ_z gives the word distribution within topic. 2) Pick a multinomial distribution θ_u for each user profile from Dirichlet distribution with parameter α. 3) Select a topic $z \in 1, ... K$ from the multinomial distribution θ_u for each word token w in user profile θ_u. 4) pick word w from the multinomial distribution ϕ_z. To generate the user profile, above procedure is repeated for N_u times where N_u is number of words in θ_u. Further, the above procedure is repeated N times for N users. The likelihood for the user profile collection is given as

$$P(u_1, ..., u_N|\alpha, \beta) = \prod_{z=1}^{K} P(\phi_z|\beta) \prod_{U=1}^{N} P(\theta_u|\alpha)(\prod_{i=1}^{N_u} \sum_{z_i=1}^{K} P(z_i|\theta)P(w_i|z_i, \phi))d\theta d\phi \tag{7}$$

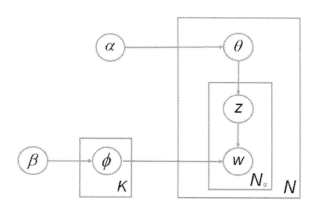

Fig. 2. User profile corpus generated by Latent Dirichlet Allocation

LDA presents a different representation compared to the language model for generating user profile based on user topics. LDA gives multiple topics for each user which shows that each user has varied interests. After we estimate θ and ϕ, the probability of generating a word from a user profile is given as

$$P_{LDA}(w|\hat{\theta}, \hat{\phi}, \theta_u) = \sum_{z=1}^{K} P(w|z, \hat{\phi})P(z|\hat{\theta}, \theta_u) \tag{8}$$

where $\hat{\theta}$ and $\hat{\phi}$ are the posterior estimates of θ and ϕ respectively.

As LDA model measures relations in the topic space rather than based on word matching, it does not require a word to appear in user profile to find correlations between a word and a specific user profile. Thus, it alleviates the lexical gap problem. Note that the value of $P_{LDA}(w|\hat{\theta}, \hat{\phi}, \theta_u)$ is used as $P_{interest}(w|\theta_u)$ in Equation 5.

4.6   Modeling User Topical Expertise

Given a new question, user who has more expertise on the question might have higher probability to be the best answerer. For each potential answerer, this expertise can be learned from his or her profile (content and voting). This expertise is defined as $P_{expertise}(w|\theta_u)$ in Equation 5.

As mentioned in Section 4.5, semantic similarity between the user profile and the new question can be captured through topic model. Therefore, we can compute $P_{expertise}(w|\theta_u)$ as

$$P_{expertise}(w|\theta_u) = P_{expertise} \sum_z P(w|z, \hat{\phi})P(z|\theta u) \tag{9}$$

where $P(w|z, \hat{\phi})$ refers to a value irrelevant to user characteristic and $P(z|\theta u)$ refers to the expertise of user u on topic z. To keep the model simple, $P(w|z, \hat{\phi})$ is computed based on the model learned in Section 4.5.

We model user topical expertise by leveraging the collaborative voting mechanism. The major challenge is to map the user's expertise on a question to his or her expertise on topics. To address this challenge, we compute the topic distribution of each answer (corresponding question is also included) from the LDA model learned in Section 4.5. Next, we distribute the user's expertise on the question to his or her expertise on topics of the question. For instance, if one question is highly related to Topic z, then expertise value for topic z will be higher as compared to other topics. The more the user answers questions related to topic z, the higher the expertise of that user has on topic z. The pseudo code for measuring user topical expertise is shown in Figure 3.

For each user in the training dataset, we use a vector EV to store his or her expertise on each topic (Line 2). For each answer given by this user, function *getScore* computes the score of the answer (together with its question) based on the votes of the answer and its accepted state (Line 6). Function *getProbability* computes the topic distribution for the question using Tassign Matrix, an output of model learned in Section 4.5 (Line 8). Tassign Matrix contains the assigned topic for each word appearing in the user profile. For instance, $QA[i]$ contains 5 words, 3 of them are assigned to topic 1 while the other 2 are assigned to topic 2. Then the topic distributions of $QA[i]$ on topic 1 and 2 are 0.6 and 0.4, respectively. Next, we distribute the score of a question based on the probability of this question for each topic (Line 9-10). After scanning QA in the user profile, we achieve EV as the user expertise on each topic, this vector is then added into the final user-topic matrix EM (Line 11). In the end, we normalize all expertise by topics to make all the absolute values of topical expertise no more than 1 (Line 12). The output matrix EM is then used in Equation 9.

Procedure LearnUserExpertise
Inputs:
  U: User Profiles
  VM: Voting Matrix, contains voting information for each answer.
  TM: Tassign Matrix
  K: Topic Number
Output:
  EM: User Topical Expertise Matrix
Methods:
  1: For each user u in U
  2:   Let EV = a vector contains u's expertise on each topic.
  3:   Let QA = answers provided by u and their corresponding questions.
  4:   For $(i = 1; i \leq |QA|; i + +)$
  5:     Let $Score$ = the expertise of u on the question $QA[i]$;
  6:     $Score = getScore(VM, u, QA[i])$
  7:     Let $Probability$ = a vector contains the topic distribution of question $QA[i]$
  8:     $Probability = getProbability(Tassign, u, QA[i])$
  9:     For $(j = 1; j \leq K; j + +)$
  10:        Add $Probability[j] \times Score$ to $EV[j]$
  11:   Add EV to EM
  12: $NormalizeByTopic(EM)$
  13: Output EM

Fig. 3. Learning user topical expertise

5   Experiment

5.1   Dataset

On StackOverflow, questions are assigned one or more tags, such as C#, Java, php, android etc. These tags are given by users to tell the category of a question. In this work, we create a dataset including questions and answers under tag C# that were posted between January 1, 2012 to December 31, 2012. We consider questions and answers under tag C# because currently C# has the highest number of questions tagged to it. Table 1 shows some basic statistics of our dataset.

Table 1. Data statistics

Tag	Questions	Askers	Answers
C#	99,166	37,363	191,338

We divide our dataset into two parts: training data and testing data. Training data include questions and answers posted from January 1, 2012 to November 30, 2012. Testing data contain questions posted from December 1, 2012 to December 31, 2012. We consider active users who have answered at least five questions during training data period as the potential answerers for testing questions.

We keep the testing questions that have an accepted answer and remove other testing questions. The answerer who gave the accepted answer to a testing question is regarded as the ground truth for that question.

5.2   Experiment Setup

User Interest Leaning. The input of the LDA model is a collection of user profiles. To learn topics' distributions on words and probabilities of user profiles generating topics, we use Gibbs sampling for inference and parameter estimation. By default, we set the number of topics as 100 and run LDA with 500 iterations of Gibbs sampling. Hyper parameters α and β are 0.5 and 0.1, respectively. Weight parameter λ is 0.5.

User Expertise Leaning. As shown in Figure 3, function *getScore* is used to compute a value for an answer to represent its quality. In the experiment, we compute this value based on the voting rules on StackOverflow: each positive vote increases the value by 10, while each negative vote reduces the value by 2. If an answer has been marked as accepted answer, we add 15 to the value of the answer.

5.3   Research Questions

RQ1: Is our method effective in predicting the best answers for new questions compared to the baseline method ? To evaluate the performance of approaches, we follow the previous related paper. Approaches need to consider all the potential answerers and rank them according to their probabilities of being the best answerer. For each testing question, if the position of the best answerer is present in a range, say among the top N (N=1,50,or 100), of the returned ranked list, we call it a success at position N. We then compute a success rate S@N by dividing the success times by the number of total testing questions.

RQ2: What is the effect of varying the parameter λ ? Our approach takes both user interest effect and user expertise effect into consideration. The parameter λ is defined in Equation 5 to control the weights of these two effects. We vary this parameter to investigate how user interest effect and user expertise effect contribute to a better ranking model.

5.4   Experiment Results

RQ1: Effectiveness of Our Approach. We compare our approach to a TF-IDF based approach. We denote our approach that combines user interest and user expertise as $Our_{Combine}$. The parameter λ is 0.5. We also consider an approach $Our_{Interest}$ which only considers user interest, i.e., the parameter λ is 0. For the evaluation metric S@N, N is varied as 1, 3, 5, 10, 20, 50, and 100. Results of these three approaches are shown in Table 2.

Table 2. Comparison of S@N rate

Approach	S@1	S@3	S@5	S@10	S@20	S@50	S@100
TF-IDF based	0.20%	0.32%	0.45%	0.65%	1.09%	2.17%	3.42%
$Our_{Interest}$	1.18%	2.14%	2.66%	3.82%	5.53%	9.226%	13.76%
$Our_{Combine}$	2.11%	4.27%	5.48%	7.76%	11.11%	16.63%	21.50%

From the results shown in Table 2 , we find that our approach $Our_{Combine}$ performs best among the three approaches. With higher values of N, we observe significant improvement in $S@N$ ratio. This result shows that our approach is more efficient in predicting the best answerers than the TF-IDF based approach. $Our_{Interest}$ approach also performs better than TF-IDF approach as $Our_{Interest}$ considers the same content as baseline approach . This result suggests that topic model might capture more information than vector space model. We also note that $Our_{Combine}$ approach is better than $Our_{Interest}$ approach, which shows that the additional information about user expertise is useful.

RQ2: Effects of Varying Parameter λ. Parameter λ defined in Equation 5 controls the impact of user interest and expertise. We range the value of λ from 0.0 to 1.0: $\lambda = 0.0$ means only consider user interest and $\lambda = 1.0$ means only consider user topical expertise. The results with different λ values are shown in Table 3.

Table 3. Varying value of parameter λ

λ	S@1	S@3	S@5	S@10	S@20	S@50	S@100
0.0	1.18%	2.14%	2.66%	3.82%	5.53%	9.226%	13.76%
0.3	2.08%	3.65%	4.74%	6.84%	9.53%	14.28%	18.92%
0.5	2.11%	4.27%	5.48%	7.76%	11.11%	16.63%	21.50%
0.7	2.14%	**4.35%**	**5.71%**	**8.38%**	11.86%	18.18%	**23.06%**
1.0	**2.18%**	4.15%	5.56%	8.33%	**12.57%**	**18.34%**	23.01%

Table 3 shows that as the value of λ increases, the success rate generally increases. The numbers in the bold highlight the highest success rate under each measurement. The setting with $\lambda = 0.7$ has the highest values for 4 out of 7 measurements, while $\lambda = 1.0$ has the highest values for the other three measurements.

5.5   Threats to Validity

Threats to internal validity refers to the representative of our model. The empirical selection of parameter like α, β, topic number K, Gibbs sampling iteration n might influence the results of LDA. We measure the quality of a question based on its votes, and the reputation rules on StackOverflow. However although the votes are given by the community, there might be human bias. For instance, user might prefer to vote up answers with more votes, or answers that are accepted, or answers given by experts.

External validity is related to the generalizability of our results. Our dataset consists of more than 99,000 questions posted from January 1, 2012 to December 31, 2012 which may not represent all the types of questions asked under category C#. Also, since we consider only questions marked under C# tag, the results may not hold true for questions belonging to other category.

Threats to construct validity corresponds to the appropriateness of the evaluation criteria. Following other similar works, we regard the user who provides the accepted answer for the test question as the ground truth based on the assumption that the answer marked as accepted has the highest equality among others. But the accepted answer is labeled by the asker, which might not be the best answer that selected by the whole community.

6   Conclusion

In this paper, we proposed an approach that combines user interest effect and user expertise effect on topic layer, to predict best answerers for new questions on Community Question Answering (CQA) sites. By using historical answered questions of users, we model the interests of the answerers using Latent Dirichlet Allocation (LDA). We also incorporate collaborative voting mechanism at CQA sites to learn user expertise on each topics. We compare the performance of our approach with the TF-IDF based approach on a dataset extracted from StackOveflow. The results show that our approach can improve the effectiveness of the baseline approach.

As a future work, we intend to expand our study to include more questions from various community question answering sites. We also plan to investigate whether we can persuade those users who do not participate actively by recommending them questions that they are interested in and have enough expertise to solve. This would mitigate the problem of low participation rate commonly faced by community question answering sites.

References

1. Liu, Y., Bian, J., Agichtein, E.: Predicting information seeker satisfaction in community question answering. In: SIGIR, pp. 483–490 (2008)
2. Liu, Q., Agichtein, E., Dror, G., Gabrilovich, E., Maarek, Y., Pelleg, D., Szpektor, I.: Predicting web searcher satisfaction with existing community-based answers. In: SIGIR, pp. 415–424 (2011)
3. Liu, X., Croft, W.B., Koll, M.B.: Finding experts in community-based question-answering services. In: CIKM, pp. 315–316 (2005)
4. Bouguessa, M., Dumoulin, B., Wang, S.: Identifying authoritative actors in question-answering forums: the case of yahoo! answers. In: KDD, pp. 866–874 (2008)

5. Qu, M., Qiu, G., He, X., Zhang, C., Wu, H., Bu, J., Chen, C.: Probabilistic question recommendation for question answering communities. In: WWW, pp. 1229–1230 (2009)
6. Liu, Q., Agichtein, E.: Modeling answerer behavior in collaborative question answering systems. In: Clough, P., Foley, C., Gurrin, C., Jones, G.J.F., Kraaij, W., Lee, H., Mudoch, V. (eds.) ECIR 2011. LNCS, vol. 6611, pp. 67–79. Springer, Heidelberg (2011)
7. Liu, M., Liu, Y., Yang, Q.: Predicting best answerers for new questions in community question answering. In: Chen, L., Tang, C., Yang, J., Gao, Y. (eds.) WAIM 2010. LNCS, vol. 6184, pp. 127–138. Springer, Heidelberg (2010)
8. Riahi, F., Zolaktaf, Z., Shafiei, M., Milios, E.: Finding expert users in community question answering. In: Proceedings of the 21st International Conference Companion on World Wide Web, pp. 791–798. ACM (2012)
9. Wang, S., Lo, D., Jiang, L.: An empirical study on developer interactions in stackoverflow. In: 28th ACM Symposium on Applied Computing (2013)
10. Xia, X., Lo, D., Wang, X., Zhou, B.: Tag recommendation in software information sites. In: Proceedings of the Tenth International Workshop on Mining Software Repositories, pp. 287–296. IEEE Press (2013)
11. Berger, A., Caruana, R., Cohn, D., Freitag, D., Mittal, V.: Bridging the lexical chasm: Statistical approaches to answer-finding. In: Proceedings of the 23rd Annual International ACM SIGIR Conference on Research and Development in Information Retrieval (2000)
12. Blei, D.M., Ng, A.Y., Jordan, M.I., Lafferty, J.: Latent dirichlet allocation. Journal of Machine Learning Research 3, 2003 (2003)

First International Workshop on Histoinformatics

(HISTOINFORMATICS 2013)

A Digital Humanities Approach to the History of Science

Eugenics Revisited in Hidden Debates by Means of Semantic Text Mining

Pim Huijnen[1], Fons Laan[2], Maarten de Rijke[2], and Toine Pieters[1]

[1] Descartes Centre for the History and Philosophy of the Sciences and the Arts,
Utrecht University, The Netherlands
{p.huijnen,t.pieters}@uu.nl
[2] ISLA, University of Amsterdam, The Netherlands
{a.c.laan,derijke}@uva.nl

Abstract. Comparative historical research on the the intensity, diversity and fluidity of public discourses has been severely hampered by the extraordinary task of manually gathering and processing large sets of opinionated data in news media in different countries. At most 50,000 documents have been systematically studied in a single comparative historical project in the subject area of heredity and eugenics. Digital techniques, like the text mining tools WAHSP and BILAND we have developed in two successive demonstrator projects, are able to perform advanced forms of multi-lingual text-mining in much larger data sets of newspapers. We describe the development and use of WAHSP and BILAND to support historical discourse analysis in large digitized news media corpora. Furthermore, we argue how text mining techniques overcome the problem of traditional historical research that only documents explicitly referring to eugenics issues and debates can be incorporated. Our tools are able to provide information on ideas and notions about heredity, genetics and eugenics that circulate in discourses that are not directly related to eugenics (e.g., sport, education and economics).

1 Introduction

The mass digitization of books, newspapers and other historical material has achieved new heights in recent years and bears the promise of exciting new possibilities for historical research. Historical scholars are increasingly incorporating computational tools and methods in all phases of their research. Digital tools are used in opening up, presenting, and curating textual and multi-media sources, in heuristic techniques of retrieval and accumulation of digitized data, in semantic text mining or geospatial information studies, in various forms of visualization and in enhanced and multi-media publications of research results, blogs, and wikis. Digital history is a methodological approach framed by the capacities of these digital tools to make, define, query, and annotate associations and analyse long term patterns of economic, technological and cultural change in the human record of the past. Digital history can be said to touch upon all aspects and forms of historical scholarship. It is not a unified field or methodology, however. It is 'an array of convergent practices' that come together around digitized data and

A. Nadamoto et al. (Eds.): SocInfo 2013 Workshops, LNCS 8359, pp. 71–85, 2014.

digital tools [18].[1] Despite inspiring examples of excellent digital historical scholarship, like mining the google books archive using ngrams [20], finding happenings 'that never happened' with the use of machine-learning, techniques [10] engaging in creative visual analysis of historical geography,[2] or studying the circulation of knowledge and learned practices by means of a virtual research environment (VRE)[3] historians have only just begun to explore what it means doing history from the perspective of both humanities and computer sciences [25, 8, 6].

Semantic text analytics is a particularly promising form of data mining that can be applied to textual data in order to derive subject-specific information out of 'mountains' of textual data without having to read it all. Text analytics or text mining is an umbrella term for incorporating and implementing a wide range of tools or techniques (algorithms, methods), including data mining, machine learning, natural language processing, and artificial intelligence. Semantic text analytics focuses specifically on the historical-contextual meanings of words and phrases in a big data set [12].

The goal of text mining is to reduce the effort required of humanities researchers to obtain useful information from large digitized text data sources. Text mining tools are able to mine and process large numbers of texts reasonably quickly and point researchers to discourses, sentiments, named entities or potentially meaningful concepts. Thus these tools help to reconstruct and analyse past mentalities. As evidently shared values, mentalities normally only surface when they are contested. After all, people's mentality consists of their values, ideals and standards and these are rarely explicit. People's worries, disputes, or what excites them are all expressions that provide an understanding of past mentalities.

Current research programs such as Digging into Data and CATCH-plus demonstrate the feasibility of performing interdisciplinary humanities research facilitated by digital research tools.[4] Adapting digital methodologies arising from these programs to humanities research gives rise to more easily reproducible results, more refined computationally-based research methods for historians, and new research questions. These programs also demonstrate that collaborative, trans-disciplinary and integrative strategies such as common group learning (all knowledge is necessarily pooled and learning is both shared and cumulative), modeling, negotiation among experts, and integration by leaders are central to the functioning and therefore the success of this approach. The design and execution of such digital humanities programs is obviously grafted on common practice in the sciences and may be contrasted to the large majority of humanities research (exceptions excluded, notably in linguistics), where research is individualistic to the core. The role of humanities experts in the field, in our case historians of science, in the development of text and data mining technology is particularly important. This applies also to articulating and aligning the needs of users with the technological options. Incorporating regular feedback loops, for instance, allows an iterative refinement of analysis algorithms and the development of a user-friendly digital tool.

---

[1] For an overview of recent trends and discussions in digital humanities see [5, 28, 1, 3].

[2] http://www.stanford.edu/group/spatialhistory (accessed 08-09-2013).

[3] http://ckcc.huygens.knaw.nl/ (accessed 08-09-2013)

[4] http://www.diggingintodata.org, http://www.catchplus.nl.

Our thesis, consequently, is that digital tools can help historians of science gain a better understanding of scientific dissemination and cultural transfer. This is what we argue in this article, as we focus on a case study of eugenics. After all, based on a wide array of undisputed scientific theories, eugenics has important cultural and political connotations around the world. In the words of Levine and Bashford, eugenics was not simply a sideline to our cultural heritage, but rather a central component of European modernity [16, 27, 17, 23, 9]. The highly problematic present connotation of the concept is an obvious heritage of the Second World War, and the racial laws under Nazi rule in particular. However, the sole focus on national-socialist race hygiene hardly does justice to the broad spectrum of meanings that eugenics has generated throughout history. Digital techniques can help to provide a better insight into the cultural meanings of eugenics.

2 Towards Historical Sentiment Mining in Public Media

2.1 WAHSP

The first step towards the development of an open source mining technology that can be used by historians without specific computer skills, is to obtain hands-on experience with research groups that use currently available open source mining tools. A recently developed tool that has been utilized to accomplish this is the CLARIN-supported web application for historical sentiment mining (a form of semantic text analytics that focuses on historical opinions, attitudes, and value judgments) in public media that is known under its acronym WAHSP.[5] WAHSP is specifically designed for text mining the digital newspaper archive of the National Library of the Netherlands. At present, this repository comprises over 10 million pages from over 200 newspapers and periodicals published between 1618 and 1995, adding up to over 100 million articles.[6]

The technical basis of WAHSP is an ElasticSearch instance combined with the xTAS text analysis service.[7] xTAS includes modules for online and offline processing. xTAS provides other essential text pre-processing modules (morphological normalization, format and encoding reconciliation, named entity recognition and normalization [19], etc.). It also incorporates algorithms and tools for identification of polarity (positive/support or negative/criticism), sources (opinion-holders), frequency of items and specific targets of discourses [13]. WAHSP comes with visualization modules built in D3.js (interactive word clouds and timelines). A statistical machine translation service is also available, which can be used to translate existing lexicons and documents between Dutch and German (both directions). The functionalities of xTAS are used to leverage interactive creation, expansion and refinement of lexicons specific to the user's research questions and needs. xTAS feeds visualizations that allow users to examine the research domain along the aforementioned dimensions of time, context, and the identity and frequency of the discourse. WAHSP has been developed in a specific research context, but is generic and usable in other domains in which analysis of topics, contexts and attitudes in large volumes of text is needed.

---

[5] http://www.clarin.nl/page/about/2; http://biland.nl
[6] The Dutch Royal Library, http://kranten.kb.nl.
[7] http://xtas.net

The main added value of the WAHSP tool lies in its possibilities for exploratory reading of historical patterns in public debates. The WAHSP research team found that, in terms of methodology, semi-automatic document selection fits rather well with historical research as an alternative to manual or random sampling, facilitating the combination of qualitative and quantitative approaches. Through text mining and visualization, new insights can be gained from an initial selection. Word clouds depicting the linguistic context within which keywords occur are instrumental in helping the historian with expert knowledge of the domain to combine and compare different historical periods in a free associative manner on the basis of a large number of historical documents. Each query immediately yields a document selection, without laborious sampling. This speeds up the heuristic process considerably. Exploring word associations and metadata, as well as visualizations of the documents over time, can lead to improved queries and, therefore, to a more representative document selection. Such quantitative analysis enhances the knowledge of the historian. A clear benefit of using exploratory searches is to allow the historian to recycle previous insights to investigate new research questions. Comparing document selections using quantitative analysis helps to validate these selections, making them less arbitrary and thus more representative.

2.2   Exploring the Meaning of Eugenics in Hidden Debates

Point of departure was the multiple discourses that converged around the use and adaptation of genetic knowledge and eugenics in the workplace, the home, and the wider world. Whereas eugenics has been the object of thorough historical research, both as an object of scientific discours and its implementation in state policies, this is not true for the dissemination of eugenic thought in society [26]. Notions of eugenics have formed—either latently or explicitly—part of modern Western culture since the rise of genetics and hereditary science. Marius Turda has defined eugenics as 'a cluster of social, biological and cultural ideas, centered on the redefinition of the individual and the national community according to the laws of natural selection and heredity' [27, p. 124] In this sense, eugenics can be seen as the (pseudo-)scientific justification of possibly traditional customs and rules within communities to keep the population 'pure' and alive. For example, rules that prohibit marriages outside a specific community have been quite common throughout history. In the sense that theories of eugenics give an explanation and a justification for these customs, one could say that eugenics is about discourse. Moreover, as eugenic notions presuppose power relations and promote inequality we understand discourse here in its Foucauldian sense.

The challenge for historians is to both qualify and quantify the impact of genetics and eugenics on culture in their historical settings and to make these power relations explicit. The ambiguities in the meaning of heredity, as mentioned above, make this type of research even more difficult. The same can be said for the fact that what is at stake here are mentalities rather than philosophies. Scientifically defined and elaborated concepts are not of primary interest for historians in this sort of cultural history (or 'history of mentalities'), but rather the unconscious, latent use of genetic or eugenic ideas by ordinary people [24].[8] For example, in the latter part of the 19th and early part

---

[8] Following Müller-Wille en Rheinberger, genetics in this sense is 'the transmission of physical properties in one generation to the other': The Production of an Epistemic Space, 11. The minimal definition is, to quote the so-titled book by Diane Paul, 'Controlling human heredity.'

of the 20th century, in a number of Western countries, there was gradually mounting public support for "hard-line" policies of eugenics, such as marriage restrictions and involuntary sterilization. In the Netherlands, however, the official eugenics movement has always been fairly marginal; thus, "hard-line" eugenics supporters were not in the position to monopolize public discourse. What did this mean for the dissemination of genetic and eugenic thinking in Dutch public discourse? What were the political and racial connotations of the arguments that circulated in newspapers and how did they become manifest in various domains—for instance: negative and positive forms of in-breeding, the growing medical interest in sports, the circus or gendered questions like what defines good motherhood? It is difficult to grasp these problems by "traditional" historical means. Digital humanities methods can be of key to help answer questions like these.

2.3 Text Mining within the Context of Tacit Knowledge

The WAHSP tool enables historians to collect and process large sets of opinion-text data from news media and extract discourse identity and intensity patterns—and to compare these patterns between different countries. The advantages above 'traditional' ways of doing historical research are clear. First, the tool enables research with no limitation on source materials. It overcomes selection issues as well as representation issues. Second, the tool makes research reproducible. Normally, an intensive research method makes it almost impossible to change or add research questions or viewpoints after analysis. One simply has to do all the work once again to ask a new question. WAHSP is made to repeat the heuristic process over and over again. Third, the tool enables research on hidden debates because one can search a combination of keywords that do not neces-sarily refer to specifically to eugenics, but rather imply eugenic thinking. Examples in-clude: 'ancestry', 'lineage', 'descent', 'stock', 'reproduction', 'regulation', 'selection', 'pure'/'purity', 'progression', 'evolvement', 'deterioration', 'depravation', 'isolation', and 'segregation'. Keyword searching is in itself not unproblematic—a rather "blunt" instrument in the words of Adrian Bingham [4, p. 229]. Finding the right keywords demands expert knowledge of the field of study and a great deal of perseverance and creativity [21, p. 67].

By combining these words with keywords from social or cultural domains like sports, circus, religion, and the like, one can obtain explicit discussions not only about eugen-ics, but also about mentalities and implicit notions influenced by hereditary and eugenic thinking within certain debates. After all, as a research object within the history of men-talities, we are not primarily interested in explicit racial and political debates influenced by genetics or eugenics. The aim of this study is, after all, to demonstrate that notions of heredity and eugenics have had an impact, no matter how diffuse or unconscious, on Dutch and German societies. Therefore, the point of departure of this research is not necessarily to identify the domains in which these debates are to be found. On the con-trary, it is the identification of these domains that is the goal of this study. An essential difference of using the WAHSP application compared to traditional scholarly methods is the tool's ability to differentiate the impact of genetics and eugenics in time and place. The tool enables the historian to make visible the relationships between "universal" sci-entific knowledge and its transfer within local contexts.

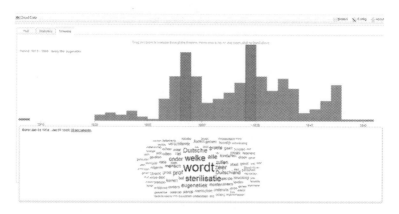

Fig. 1. WAHSP search result plus additional word cloud based on KB newspaper repository using query 'eugenetiek' ('eugenics') for 1900–1940. Bursts are indicated in red.

Like the "traditional" historian's craftsmanship, using the WAHSP tool starts with a comprehensive overview of the field of study. Detailed knowledge of contemporary science and fashionable cultural concerns within distinct historical settings enables the researcher to formulate a number of research questions. These are turned into queries that consist of carefully selected keywords—like the examples mentioned above. In addition to keywords, a query can include a specific time period, a particular document source, or any combination of these. Working with a limitless number of queries (in theory) removes the limitation of having a single sampling strategy.

Although the WAHSP tool offers a number of options for quantitative analysis, such as the frequency of words or combinations of words used in specific newspaper articles in a certain period of time, it derives its most promising analytical potential from its visualization and arrangement features. Each query results in a term cloud that is based on the relative frequencies of the words occurring in the retrieved selection of documents from the corpus (Fig. 1). The visualization of word associations in these term clouds allows the historian, on the basis of existing domain expertise, to quickly determine the characteristics of the selected documents, and to refine or adapt the query. Also, WAHSP is able to indicate sentiments by highlighting terms with a negative or positive connotation, but it should be noted that this technique of sentiment detection is still in need of historical contextualization and linguistic fine-tuning. We decided not to include the sentiment mining in our historical research for reasons of insufficient validity. Techniques for named entity recognition (Fig. 2), however, enable the researcher to recognize and highlight the names of 'entities' such as places, persons, institutions, and events. This tool allows the historian to place the occurrence of certain terms, ideas, or debates within a geographical context, or connect them to persons or organizations.

Lastly, a visualization of the temporal distribution of the documents allows the historian to discover patterns in publication dates. This visualization is a histogram plot of publication dates that can be explored interactively (Fig. 1); zooming in on specific parts of the histogram provides finer-grained data. To enable quick recognition of atypical patterns, bursts within the histogram—time periods where significantly more

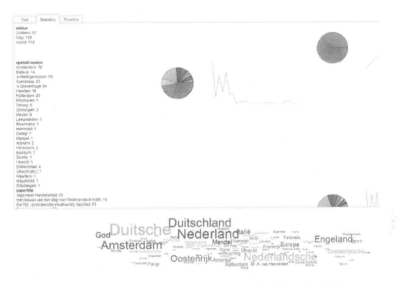

Fig. 2. WAHSP search result with named entity recognition cloud based on KB newspaper repository using query 'eugenetiek' ('eugenics') for 1900–1940

documents were published in comparison to periods around that burst are highlighted. Clicking on a burst yields a visualization of word associations of that burst alone and a list of documents contained within that burst. At any point in time the historian can return to the original text of the newspaper article. This allows the historian to get an in-depth understanding of what each burst is about. Together, these interactions allow historians to interactively investigate the document selection in order to detect patterns, improving the representativeness of the selection [22].

3   Case Studies

3.1   Exploratory Search

Self-acclaimed eugenicists were the strongest believers and successful advocates of eugenics laws and practices, as the history of many countries has shown. One reason why "hard-line" eugenics-supporters were not in the position to monopolize public discourse in the Netherlands was the absence of a strong eugenics movement. There was a strong social opposition against measures based upon eugenic notions like segregation, forced castration or sterilization. However, this opposition had more to do with a principal aversion against state intervention in what were considered private affairs than with moral problems with eugenics as such. Therefore, it remains interesting to know if the absence of eugenic practices means that eugenic thinking was absent altogether in the Netherlands.

The WAHSP tool is able to localize distinct cultural domains and public discourses that did not openly flirt with hard-line genetics, but yet had definite notions of genetic and eugenic thinking. The hints of eugenic notions in pre-war Dutch economic debates

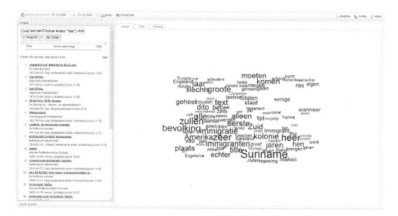

Fig. 3. WAHSP search result plus word cloud based on the KB newspaper repository using the query 'race' AND 'immigration' ('ras' AND 'immigratie') for 1860–1945. The words 'Amerika' and 'Amerikaansche' ('America' and 'American') both form part of the cloud, indicating at the reference to the US in articles that contain both query keywords.

can serve as an example—one that, moreover, has turned out to be highly suitable to illustrate what we mean by exploratory search methods. The Princeton based economic historian Thomas C. Leonard argues how Progressive Era (ca. 1890-1920s) economists have advocated the minimum wage in the US as a eugenic tool. It would cause job losses and, as a consequence, it would discourage prospective immigrants to the US, as well as remove from employment the more unfit (the so-called "low wage races"): "The minimum wage protects deserving workers from the competition of the unfit by making it illegal to work for less" [15, 14, p. 213]. It is an interesting question whether similar arguments were used in Dutch debates on minimum wage. The Netherlands did not adopt a general minimum wage before 1968. Nonetheless, the introduction of a minimum wage was debated from as early as the turn of the 20th century. The WAHSP tool generates almost 10,000 hits on 'minimum wage' before 1945. These, obviously, also include the instances where Dutch newspapers reflect on foreign debates. But this is exactly what we are looking for: whether the Dutch debate on minimum wage was subjective to eugenic arguments from abroad—notably from the US. There are several exploratory angles to address this question. One can, for instance, query (combinations of) relevant keywords that characterize this particular debate ('race', '(minimum) wage', 'immigration' and the like) or look for a possible link with the US. The combination 'race AND immigration', for example, hints at a connection with the US. 'Amerika' ('America') and 'Amerikaansche' ('American') both appear in the cloud generated from the 184 hits (Fig. 3). Moreover, both the combinations 'wage AND race' and 'wage AND immigration' yield relative high numbers of hits (respectively more than 9,000 and almost 2,500).

We operationalize exploratory search as the ongoing combination of keywords in ways that are perhaps 'shallow' in terms of text mining techniques, but demand the most of scholarly expertise and creativity. Word clouds themselves are an important part of this search method, because striking words can trigger the researcher to incorporate them in new queries. The key question derived from this method is: what do the results tell us? They seem to indicate a meaningful connection between the concepts of race, wage and immigration in the Netherlands before the Second World War. The relatively large numbers of hits resulting from queries with combinations from these keywords, are tempting clues to investigate this particular topic further. After all, it is obvious that the results from these queries in themselves do not give any outcome about the ways in which these concepts were significantly connected. The researcher has to assess this by further research: digitally, with the use of a more elaborate text mining procedure, but also always by 'traditional' close reading of relevant texts.

3.2   Quantifying and Contextualizing Concepts or Ideas

To open new options in the heuristic processes is not the only use for text mining tools. A perhaps unspectacular, but still noteworthy and important angle for text mining is confirmatory searching. Tools like WAHSP can help to support existing narratives. Traditionally, arguments for historical narratives are commonly found in reports, correspondence or manifests—i.e., in sources in which motives are generally explicated. Relying on these sources always means taking into account justifications or propaganda. This is less the case in text mining. The newspapers corpora in which the WAHSP tool searches are, obviously, by no means unbiased. However, generating results from large numbers of texts tends to lessen the effects of particular opinions. Moreover, the WAHSP tool is able to extract implicit notions and assumptions from its sources. By doing so, it bypasses biases in these sources altogether. For example, before WWII the Dutch 'special education' domain was surrounded by a discourse that clearly evokes associations with eugenic or at least discriminatory thinking. For children in the special education system—i.e., 'weak', 'sick' or 'poor' children—'colonies' were built where they could retreat for a period of time to gain strength [2]. Although commonly refuted by historians, it remains an interesting question whether the isolation and segregation of certain hereditary traits that were considered negative were central to the establishment of these private facilities. However, in this case WAHSP confirms the master narrative in every way. In no way do queries from the 'special education' domain yield results that can be linked to hereditary thinking. This supports the thesis that 'poor relief' motives for facilities for 'unfit' children were no mere justifications, but the result of sincere intentions.

The use of digital tools to confirm existing historical knowledge in this way may seem superfluous. However, it is our opinion that it is not the sole purpose of scholarly research to prove existing ideas false. To confirm present knowledge in new, quantitative, ways certainly has a value. Moreover, the use of digital tools in this sense has a significance of its own. It may help to get the use of these tools accepted as an additional means for historical research by the scholarly community. Besides, confirmatory results advantage the further development of these tool themselves, as Frederick W. Gibbs and Trevor J. Owens have stated: "As humanists continue to prove that data manipulation and machine learning can confirm existing knowledge, such techniques come closer to telling us something we don't already know" [7].

One way of generating new knowledge is the ability of text mining to study the history of ideas and concepts (*Begriffsgeschichte*) in new ways. WAHSP is able to quantify

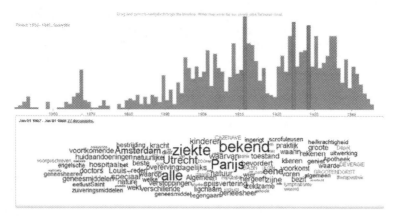

Fig. 4. WAHSP search result in the form of a timeline from the query 'inheritance' ('erfelijkheid') for 1860–1945 and an additional word cloud for the year 1867. The large number of words pointing at the medical sphere ('doctors', 'hospitaal', 'geneesmiddelen', 'geneesheeren', 'apotheek', 'heilkrachtigheid' etc.) gives a hint of the context with which this concept predominantly was connected.

and contextualize the historical uses of concepts. This involves a far more straightforward use of the text mining tool than its more intuitive heuristic use. E.g., mining the concept of 'inheritance', WAHSP can yield a timeline that indicates the frequency of the word in newspaper articles. Given the ambiguous meanings of the word 'inheritance'—referring, e.g., not only to heredity, but also to legal and cultural forms of heritage—the tool can indicate the dominant contexts in which the concept appeared from year to year. In this instance, the WAHSP tool clearly demonstrates that the biological meaning of inheritance was dominant throughout the end of the 19th and the first half of the 20th century. However, the context in which the concept was debated did change considerably over time. E.g., the word cloud makes it plainly visible that articles containing the word 'inheritance', in 1867, predominantly focused on medical subjects (Fig. 4). In 1935, however, the medical context of inheritance has almost completely been replaced by a legal and racial context (Fig. 5).

In its relative straightforwardness, the quantification and contextualization that text mining provides offer an innovative contribution to the history of ideas and concepts.[9] Timelines like the ones created by the WAHSP tool show when concepts came into use, point at frequency increases and decreases and at a concept's final disappearance. Also, the changing word clouds over time indicate the shifting contexts in which concepts were debated, thus pointing towards the varying meanings of the words in question.

3.3   New Horizons: Historical Text Mining for Comparative Research

As a follow-up of the WAHSP-project the bilingual text mining tool BILAND is currently being developed as an open-source and accessible web application. An interdisciplinary

---

[9] As Peter Haber argues in his overview of the Digital Humanities on Docupedia-Zeitgeschichte: https://docupedia.de/zg/Digital_Humanities (24-01-2013).

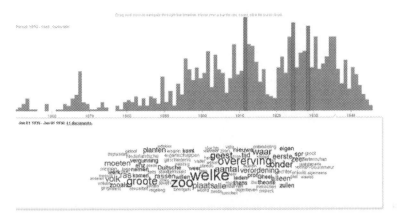

Fig. 5. WAHSP search result in the form of a timeline from the query 'inheritance' ('erfelijkheid') for 1860–1945 and an additional word cloud for the year 1935. The medical words have disappeared. Instead, 'inheritance' is much more linked to a racial context: 'volk', 'ras', 'vergunning', 'verordening', etc.

team of researchers are tailoring WAHSP to the language-specific needs of comparative historical research, with a particular focus on the identity, intensity, and location of discourses about heredity, genetics, and eugenics in Dutch and German newspapers between 1863 and 1940. The challenge is to incorporate the semantics of two different languages (in this case Dutch and German). As in WAHSP, BILAND employs a user-oriented, iterative model of collaboration between humanities scholars and ICT developers.

Comparative, bilingual historical text mining evokes a range of challenges. An important question is the comparability of the research topic as it is formulated in a specific query. The national vocabularies may not be literally translatable, as is, for example, the case for 'eugenics.' Whereas the Dutch terminology follows the English—'eugenetica,' 'eugeniek'—in the German language the most common translation for 'eugenics' is 'Rassenhygiene' ('racial hygiene'). The more literal translation 'Eugenik' did exist, and was used in the same sense, but would by itself in no way be a sufficient keyword to look for eugenic thought in Germany. In this specific kind of historical text mining it is, therefore, all the more important to be aware of what it is that is compared: a word (as shown in Fig. 6) or a concept, i.e., the meaning behind that word.

Besides the comparability of historical concepts the possibility of comparison between the given data sets also must be questioned. Do they represent a similar historical entity—the 'people', the 'public debate' (in an ideal situation)? In our media history case study: is an equal range of newspapers represented in the data set that were published in a given period? Did these newspapers have a similar coverage among the public? Is there a comparable balance between national and regional newspapers, between newspapers representing urban and those representing country regions, etc.? In BILAND, the comparability is way off. Because of IPR problems and the lack of useful digitized newspaper archives, the only digitized newspaper archive from Germany the project was able to use was the *Amtspresse Preussens*.[10] This dataset comprises of three

---

[10] http://zefys.staatsbibliothek-berlin.de/amtspresse

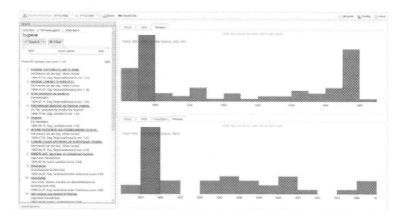

Fig. 6. BILAND search result in the form of two timelines from the query 'hygiene' for 1860-1900. The Dutch timeline is shown on top, the German below.

19th century newspapers,[11] together containing less than 20,000 digitized pages. These are hardly comparable to the Dutch data set of 10 million pages, not only in quantity, but also in the time period covered and the national scope. The German national libraries are, however, rapidly catching up. They have initiated several digitizing projects, e.g., within the Europeana[12] community.

Despite the urgency of these challenges, the use of text mining techniques holds the promise of an innovative and exciting method for comparative historical research as well. In principle, it is able to address the history of concepts and of mentalities in creative new ways. It can point at concurrences or transfers of ideas, beliefs or knowledge that traditional historical research is not able to do. Fig. 6, for example, shows the concurrence of the word 'hygiene'[13] in both Dutch and German datasets. Without ignoring the usual problems of historical comparison, the burst in 1863 in both sets of historical newspapers is exciting enough to continue this line of research.

4   Conclusion

In a recent blog post called 'The Deceptions of Data', Andrew Prescott has criticized the jubilation of the 'digital revolution'. He states that "One of the problems confronting data enthusiasts in the humanities is that we feel a need to convince our more old-fashioned colleagues about what can be done. But our role as advocates of digitized data shouldn't mean that we lose our critical sense as scholars. [...] [T]here is a risk that we look more carefully at the technical components of the datasets than the historical context of the information that they represent."[14] The quintessence of Prescott's warning

---

[11] Provinzial Correspondenz (1863–1884), Neueste Mittheilungen (1882–1894) and Teltower Kreisblatt (1856–1896).

[12] http://www.europeana.eu/

[13] In Dutch: 'hygiëne', in German: 'Hygiene'.

[14] http://digitalriffs.blogspot.nl/2013/01/
the-deceptions-of-data.html

is not to expect computer-generated conclusions of digital history and no machine-learned substitution for historical craftsmanship.

However, this does not mean digital techniques have little value for historians. Digital tools enable historians to analyze massive volumes of texts and other big data sets and to integrate (socio-) linguistics, statistics and geo-informatics into historical research. New techniques of large-scale data analysis allow historians to manage data sets that were only accessible by means of manual sampling. Exploratory search methods that are able to provide a quick overview combined with tools to zoom into details are especially empowering. Our proposed combination of interactive exploratory search and text mining supports historians to set up systematic search trails; the tooling helps them interpret and contrast the returned result sets: by exploring word associations for a result set, inspecting the temporal distribution of documents and by comparing selections historians can make a more informed and principled document selection. Obviously, this is no substitute for the historical workmanship. WAHSP and BILAND are meant as heuristic tools that ideally inspire new ideas and insights that would not have been generated through reading a small number of articles, but instead are only brought forth through the analysis of hundreds of articles. These insights may help to frame new research questions, thus catalyzing historical research [7]. They may help to frame new research questions, but also to stimulate serendipity. After all, digitally produced results often lead to unexpected associations that turn out promising for further research.

However, there are a number of prerequisites for the use of digital tools becoming standard procedure in historical research. First, it is quintessential that historians working with digital tools and building their arguments on digital results are highly aware of what they are doing. This may sound obvious, but it is hardly always the case. Historians should have a clear understanding of, for example, what word clouds are standing for. Or of how to translate complex queries into normal, everyday language. They should be able to interpret and explain text mining research results in formulations such as, 'within the given source material, in all articles containing word x and word y, word z also appears with a significant frequency'. This makes their arguments transparent. As long as digital tools are treated as black boxes, with queries going in and several sorts of visualizations mysteriously coming out, the assessment of the results remains problematic. It is therefore that Gibbs and Owens argue that "[t]he processes for working with the vast amounts of easily accessible and diverse large sets of data suggest a need for historians to formulate, articulate, and propagate ideas about how data should be approached in historical research" [7]. In parallel, a thorough understanding should be developed of the search behavior of historians, in the same vain as [11].

It is essential that the status of the results from digital tools is clearly communicated. Evidently, tools like WAHSP and BILAND offer proof for certain arguments, but do not provide explanations for them. Fore-mentioned applications can show that in the Dutch public debate at the end of the 19th century, the predominant meaning of the concept of inheritance was medical, but it does not explain why.

In sum, text mining tools like WAHSP and BILAND are not built to make writing histories abundant. They are meant to trigger historians, to draw their attention to potentially interesting cases to explore. In this sense, it is evident that text mining can form a relevant addition to the historian's toolbox outside the eugenics cases as well. It can be used to analyze trends and patterns on a much broader scale.

Acknowledgments. This research was supported by the European Community's Seventh Framework Programme (FP7/2007-2013) under grant agreement nr 288024 (LiMoSINe project), the Netherlands Organisation for Scientific Research (NWO) under project nrs 640.004.802, 727.011.005, 612.001.116, HOR-11-10, the Center for Creation, Content and Technology (CCCT), the BILAND and QuaMerdes projects funded by the CLARIN-nl program, the TROVe project funded by the CLARIAH program, the Dutch national program COMMIT, the ESF Research Network Program ELIAS, the Elite Network Shifts project funded by the Royal Dutch Academy of Sciences (KNAW), the Netherlands eScience Center under project number 027.012.105 and the Yahoo! Faculty Research and Engagement Program.

References

[1] Burdick., A., et al.: Digital Humanities. MIT Press (2012)
[2] Bakker, N.: "Kweekplaatsen van gezondheid". Vakantiecolonies en de medicalisering van het kinderwelzijn. Low Countries Historical Review 126, 29–53 (2011)
[3] Berry, D.M. (ed.): Understanding Digital Humanities. Palgrave Macmillan (2012)
[4] Bingham, A.: The digitization of newspaper archives: Opportunities and challenges for historians. Twentieth Century British History 21(2), 225–231 (2010)
[5] Earheart, A.E., Jewell, A. (eds.): The American Literature Scholar in the Digital Age. University of Michigan Press (2011)
[6] van Eijnatten, J., Pieters, T., Verheul, J.: Big data for global history: The transformative promise of digital humanities. In: BMGN (forthcoming, 2014)
[7] Gibbs, F., Owens, T.: The hermeneutics of data and historical writing (2012), http://writinghistory.trincoll.edu/data/gibbs-owens-2012-spring/
[8] Graham, S., Milligan, I., Weingart, S.: The hermeneutics of data and historical writing. In: The Historian's Macroscope: Big Digital History. Imperial College Press (2013)
[9] Hahn, D.: Modernisierung und Biopolitik: Sterilisation und Schwangerschaftsabbruch in Deutschland nach 1945. Campus (2000)
[10] van den Hoven, M., van den Bosch, A., Zervanou, K.: Beyond reported history: Strikes that never happened. In: Darányi, S., Lendvai, P. (eds.) Proceedings of the First International AMICUS Workshop on Automated Motif Discovery in Cultural Heritage and Scientific Communication Texts, Vienna, Austria, pp. 20–28 (2010)
[11] Huurnink, B., Hollink, L., van den Heuvel, W., de Rijke, M.: Search behavior of media professionals at an audiovisual archive: A transaction log analysis. Journal of the American Society for Information Science and Technology 61(6), 1180–1197 (2010)
[12] Jackson, P., Moulinier, I.: Natural Language Processing for Online Applications: Text Retrieval, Extraction and Categorization, 2nd edn. John Benjamins (2007)
[13] Jijkoun, V., de Rijke, M., Weerkamp, W.: Generating focused topic-specific sentiment lexicons. In: ACL 2010 (2010)
[14] Klausen, S., Bashford, A.: Fertility control: Eugenics, neo-malthusianism, and feminism. In: Bashford, A., Levine, S. (eds.) The Oxford Handbook of the History of Eugenics, pp. 98–115. Oxford University Press (2010)
[15] Leonard, T.C.: Eugenics and economics in the progressive era. Journal of Economic Perspectives 19, 207–224 (2005)

[16] Levine, P., Bashford, A.: Introduction: Eugenics and the modern world. In: Levine, P., Bashford, A. (eds.) The Oxford Handbook of the History of Eugenics, Oxford, pp. 3–24 (2010)

[17] Lombardo, P. (ed.): A Century of Eugenics in America: from the Indiana Experiment to the Human Genome Era. Indiana University Press (2001)

[18] Lunenfeld, P., Presner, T., Schnapp, J.: Digital humanities manifesto 2.0 (2009), http://hastac.org/node/2182

[19] Meij, E., Bron, M., Hollink, L., Huurnink, B., de Rijke, M.: Learning semantic query suggestions. In: Bernstein, A., Karger, D.R., Heath, T., Feigenbaum, L., Maynard, D., Motta, E., Thirunarayan, K. (eds.) ISWC 2009. LNCS, vol. 5823, pp. 424–440. Springer, Heidelberg (2009)

[20] Michel, J.B.: Quantitative analysis of culture using millions of digitized books. Science 6014, 176–183 (2010)

[21] Nicholson, B.: The digital turn. Media History 19(1), 59–73 (2013)

[22] Odijk, D., de Rooij, O., Peetz, M.-H., Pieters, T., de Rijke, M., Snelders, S.: Semantic document selection. Historical research on collections that span multiple centuries. In: Zaphiris, P., Buchanan, G., Rasmussen, E., Loizides, F. (eds.) TPDL 2012. LNCS, vol. 7489, pp. 215–221. Springer, Heidelberg (2012)

[23] Reulecke, J. (ed.): Herausforderung Bevölkerung: zu Entwicklungen des modernen Denkens über die Bevölkerung vor, im und nach dem 'Dritten Reich'. VS Verlag für Sozialwissenschaften (2007)

[24] Rheinberger, H.J., McLaughlin, P., Müller-Wille, S.: Introduction. In: A Cultural History of Heredity I, 17th and 18th Century, pp. 1–5. Preprint MPIWG, Berlin (2001)

[25] Seefeldt, D., Thomas III, W.G.: What is digital history? A look at some exemplar projects. Faculty Publications, Department of History. Paper 98 (2009), http://digitalcommons.unl.edu/historyfacpub/9

[26] Snelders, S., Pieters, T.: Van degeneratie tot individuele gezondheidsopties: Het maatschappelijk gebruik van erfelijkheidsconcepten in de twintigste eeuw. Gewina 26(4), 203–215 (2003)

[27] Turda, M.: Modernism and Eugenics. Palgrave MacMillan (2010)

[28] Warwick, C., Terras, M.M., Nyhan, J.: Digital Humanities in Practice. Facet (2012)

Building the Social Graph of the History of European Integration

A Pipeline for Humanist-Machine Interaction in the Digital Humanities

Lars Wieneke[1], Marten Düring[1], Ghislain Silaume[1], Carine Lallemand[2],
Vincenzo Croce[3], Marilena Lazzarro[3], Francesco Nucci[3], Chiara Pasini[4],
Piero Fraternali[4], Marco Tagliasacchi[4], Mark Melenhorst[5], Jasminko Novak[6],
Isabel Micheel[6], Erik Harloff[6], and Javier Garcia Moron[7]

[1] Centre Virtuel de la Connaissance sur l'Europe
Château de Sanem L-4992 Sanem G.-D. Luxembourg
{Lars.Wieneke,Marten.Duering,Ghislain.Sillaume}@cvce.eu
[2] Public Research Centre Henri Tudor
29 avenue John F. Kennedy L-1855 Luxembourg
Carine.Lallemand@tudor.lu
[3] Engineering Ingegneria Informatica S.p.a.
via S.Martino della battagli, 56 – Rome, Italy
{Vincenzo.Croce,Marilena.Lazzaro,Francesco.Nucci}@eng.it
[4] Dipartimento di Elettronica, Informazione e Bioingegneria
Politecnico di Milano, Piazza Leonardo da Vinci, 32, 20133 Milano, Italy
{pasini,fraternali,tagliasacchi}@elet.polimi.it
[5] Delft University of Technology
P.O. Box 5, 2600 AA Delft, The Netherlands
m.s.melenhorst@tudelft.nl
[6] European Institute for Participatory Media
Wilhelmstr. 67, 10117 Berlin, Germany
{e.harloff,i.micheel,j.novak}@eipcm.org
[7] Homeria Open Solutions S.L.
Edificio Tajo de Gestión del Conocimiento
Avenida Universidad, s/n, CP 10003 Cáceves, Spain
javiergarcia@homeria.com

Abstract. The breadth and scale of multimedia archives provides a tremendous potential for historical research that hasn't been fully tapped up to know. In this paper we want to discuss the approach taken by the History of Europe application, a demonstrator for the integration of human and machine computation that combines the power of face recognition technology with two distinctively different crowd-sourcing approaches to compute co-occurrences of persons in historical image sets. These co-occurrences are turned into a social graph that connects persons with each other and positions them, through information about the date and location of recording, in time and space. The resulting visualization of the graph as well as analytical tools can help

A. Nadamoto et al. (Eds.): SocInfo 2013 Workshops, LNCS 8359, pp. 86–99, 2014.

historians to find new impulses for research and to un-earth previously unknown relationships. As such the integration of human expertise and machine computation enables a new class of applications for the exploration of multimedia archives with significant potential for the digital humanities.

Keywords: Face recognition, Entity linking, User centered design, Data visualization, Digital Humanities, Human-machine Interaction, History, European Studies.

1   Introduction

With the increasing digitalization of contemporary historical sources, such as images, videos or sound recordings, new opportunities for research emerge.[1] Nevertheless, automatic processes alone are often not reliable enough to extract high-level information, such as the identity of persons that are depicted in these resources. A fully manual validation of faces and identities on the other hand creates highly reliable information but leads at the same time to a bottleneck for the indexation of larger archives. Moreover, most media archives co-exist independently of each other and make cross-referencing of their contents difficult. In this paper we want to discuss how the History of Europe (HoE) application overcomes these limitations through an adapted combination of human and machine computation that creates synergies between the effectiveness of automated systems and the expertise of (expert) crowd wisdom.

Up until now the full potential of such combinations remains largely untapped due to the complexity and diverse demands of such projects: The implementation and integration of processing and recognition algorithms requires specialized know-how and users from the humanities are challenged with expressing requirements for unprecedented tasks and methods which haven't emerged yet while the final application should be useable for users who don't have a technical background. To overcome these issues HoE follows a decidedly user-centered approach that tries to fuse research in computer science, the design of human-computation tasks, data visualization, social engineering and the humanities in a coherent application.

To do the complexity of the process justice it is the goal of this paper not only to describe the current (technological) state of the HoE app and to give an outlook on its future development but also to highlight the development process itself.

The HoE app overcomes the inherent complexity of hybrid human and machine computation in part through its integration in the CUbRIK framework. CUbRIK[2] is an FP7-ICT funded 36-month long project that started in October 2011 and which

---

[1] The CUbRIK consortium, parts of which have authored this paper together, is grateful for the funding received through the European Community's Seventh Framework Program FP7-ICT, Grant agreement no: 287704.
[2] See http://www.cubrikproject.eu/

focuses on building a flexible platform for multimedia search that combines human input and machine computation. The second chapter of this paper therefore gives a brief introduction into the architecture of the CUbRIK platform to provide a context for the further development of the HoE app.

In chapter three, *From idea to requirements*, the specification process is described as a mediation between *user pull* and *technology push*. In contrast to common software development processes which follow a specific need expressed by the final users, the initial impulse for the development of HoE emerged from the CUbRIK project for which HoE serves as a demonstrator application. The section will highlight how this strong *technology push* has been turned in an input for a group of humanities researchers during a focus group at the Centre Virtuel de la Connaissance sur l'Europe (CVCE) in Luxembourg and how in turn the feedback of these experts was taken as an input for a feasibility review that led to the final concept for the HoE application.

Chapter four describes the different components of the HoE app in more detail. After a discussion of the image indexation pipeline and its two different approaches to crowdsourcing through the integration of both click-workers and an expert crowd, first the construction and finally the visualization of the social graph is presented.

The fifth chapter on *Expert sourcing and user motivation* discusses how to involve communities of experts in crowdsourcing tasks that would be too difficult to solve for non-expert users. The section starts off with a description of the general challenges for crowdsourcing, followed by the specific role of experts in the HoE app. It continues with an excursus on the nature of truth in science and the humanities. Untypical for computer science but very typical for the humanities we will discuss how the HoE app tries to enable competing interpretations of historical "facts" through the integration of multiple perspectives in the user interface rather relying only on binary opositions. The chapter concludes with a review of different types of user motivations and derived incentives as well as their integration in the interface.

Finally the paper will give an outlook on the future development of the HoE app.

2   From CUbRIK to the History of Europe Application

The CUbRIK approach facilitates the interaction between human input and machine computations. From the ground up CUbRIK has been designed to be a flexible platform that could be tailored to meet the specific needs of different domains. As a whole the CUBRIK platform is built for multimedia search practitioners, researchers and end-users and relies on a framework for executing processes (the so called CUbRIK pipelines), which bundle and distribute the tasks to be executed. The original concept for the CUBRIK architecture is specified in Figure 1.

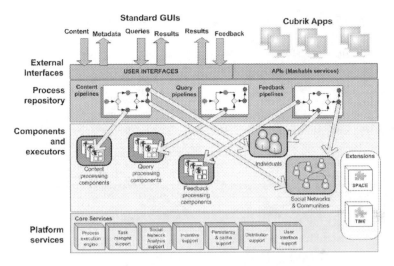

Fig. 1. Key components of the CUbRIK architecture

Each CUbRIK pipeline is described by a workflow of tasks, allocated to executors. Task executors can be software components for data analysis, metadata indexing, search engines and the presentation of results among others. Moreover, tasks can also be allocated to human users, for example via gaming interfaces, or to an entire community, for example by a crowdsourcing tool component.

This idea reflects the CUbRIK approach to have *Humans in the loop* of generic search processes. Human activities can involve both humans playing GWAPs [3] and crowdsourcing markets[4] via frameworks like Amazon Mechanical Turk[5] or Microtask[6].

3   From Idea to Requirements

The CUbRIK project is characterized by a strong interplay between technological progress and the development of applications that are tailored to the needs of end-users. Throughout the project, efforts have been made to elicit the needs of end-users and use their input for the requirements specification process. This can be referred to as 'user pull'.

Simultaneously, solutions have been developed that combine machine-based processing with human and social intelligence. In order to assess the added value of these solutions, an application environment is needed that allows for the technical evaluation of the solutions. This is referred to as 'technology push'.

---

[3] GWAP – Games With A Purpose is the CUbRIK gamification strategy to outsource certain processes to humans while also being entertaining.
[4] The crowdsourcing market outsources tasks to a crowd of paid workers.
[5] https://www.mturk.com
[6] http://www.microtask.com/

Following a combined 'user pull' and 'technology push'' approach (see Figure 2), the resulting application should then contain new technology that demonstrates the added value of combining machine-based processing with human and social intelligence, while it simultaneously should make it easier for historians to explore and annotate historical sources. The process of mapping these solutions to the needs of historians (and vice versa) involves an estimation of technical feasibility and alignment of different components. During this mapping process, researchers in Human Computer Interaction therefore worked closely together with multimedia information retrieval specialists.

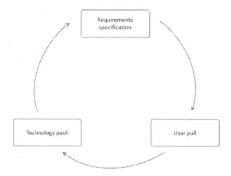

Fig. 2. The role of user pull and technology push in specifying requirements

The following steps were taken in order to combine support for the work of historians with advanced multimedia search technologies. Initially, five different user stories were developed, each describing both a task the domain experts perform as part of their daily research work, and a technological solution to support the task at hand. The user stories were evaluated with a focus group of domain experts as the future end users, an expert in the field of multimedia search and retrieval as well as CUbRIK's technical experts, the latter considering technical feasibility and relevance to the CUbRIK project.

Additionally, two exploratory interviews were conducted to get a specific idea about the work of the domain experts, its complexity, and the experts' needs for support. As a result, user stories that were both challenging from a technological perspective and promising from the point of view of the expert users were selected for further refinement.

The selection of user stories initiated the application specification process, including the design of mock-ups for each of the user stories. The mock-ups fulfilled two functions: 1) to visualize the needed features, and hence to assist the technical specification process; 2) to demonstrate what the experts would actually do with our ideas and how the application would fit into their workflow.

A second focus group with 5 CVCE-experts was set up to improve our understanding of the historians' needs, and foremost, to collect feedback on the mock-ups and the concepts behind them. The results led to modifications of the mock-ups and provided further input for the technical requirements specification process, both of which will be the basis for the CUbRIK History of Europe application.

In order to be able to evaluate whether the formulated requirements have been met, a set of success criteria has been specified, relating to both the technical performance of the pipelines that are used in the application (system oriented evaluation) as well as the extent to which the application offers added value to the history experts and how the experts evaluate the user experience (user-based evaluation). The set of success criteria will be the basis for the set up of both the system-oriented evaluation and the user-based evaluation.

4   The History of Europe Application

The History of Europe (HoE) application is - at this early stage in its development - based on a curated collection of more than 3000 images, representing the main events and actors in the history of the European integration. Other collections of relevant digitized sources, for example from the Europeana archive will be added to the app and processed using the CUbRIK pipeline. The current collection is curated and hosted by the CVCE.

In a first step, an image indexation pipeline identifies the location of individual faces in the photographs. The location of these faces is verified by a crowd of "click-workers" with no specific training who evaluate for each recognized face if the depicted image shows a human face or not. Following the face verification process, an automatic face recognition process is triggered that associates each of the now verified faces with a list of ten possible identities. This list of candidates is then disseminated to a crowd of experts that vote and comment for their preferred identity.

Besides the identities of the different persons, all information that is associated to an image, such as the time or the place where the image was taken as well as contextual information about associated historical events can be reviewed by expert users and delegated to a crowd of domain experts for review. Links between historical actors can already be explored using the Social graph. Building on the computed co-occurrence of persons in images a network visualization is constructed which connects them to each other. At this stage, connections gain in strength the more often persons appear together in an image (see 4.2).

4.1   Image Indexation - The CUbRIK Pipeline

Images go through a pipeline that seamlessly integrates algorithms executed by a computer with human-executed tasks. Each image is scanned searching for persons, by means of a state-of-the art face detection/recognition automatic tool[7]. This task is particularly challenging given the diversity in the quality of photographs taken between the 1950s and the present as well as by the process of aging of those who they depict. The tool consists of two basic components: the first devoted to face detection and the second to face identification. First, the face detection component receives as input a collection of images that are analyzed one by one. Once a photo is

---

[7] Kee Square, Morpheus SDK, http://www.keesquare.com/htmldoc/

processed, the detector provides as output a collection of bounding boxes (i.e., regions of the image in which a face is detected). For each detected face the component provides: i) additional information pertaining the pose of the face; ii) the confidence score of the detection. Due to the challenging nature of the images contained in the dataset (e.g., non-frontal faces, shading, occlusions, etc.) the output of the detector contains both false positives (i.e., bounding boxes identifying regions in which no faces appear) and false negatives (i.e., some of the faces are not detected). For this reason, a crowdsourcing solution is employed to correct for these errors, leveraging a crowd of non-expert users.

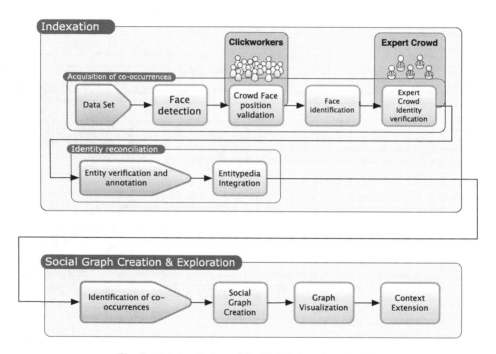

Fig. 3. High-level view of the HoE indexation pipeline

At the end of the detection phase, the face identification component extracts a biometric template from each detected bounding box. Then, a similarity score is computed between the biometric template of each unknown face and those of already known persons, which are included in an initial dataset enriched with portraits of persons whose names were known and validated by experts beforehand. If more than one reference template is available for a known person, the largest similarity score is retained. Then, for each unknown face, a ranked list is produced in decreasing order of the similarity score. In our experiments with more than 200 known persons in the initial dataset, the top-1 element represented the correct person in 18% of the cases. In 39% of the cases the correct person was listed among the top-10 elements. Therefore, a second crowdsourcing task is performed to correctly assign the identity to each unknown face. In this case, an expert is asked to select one person in a list of 10 suggested names, or indicate another person if her/his name is not included in the suggestions.

At the end of this process, an identified person is assigned to its appropriate entity in Entitypedia, a repository for linked data on historical events and people[8]. This allows us to map a person's appearance in different images unambiguously to only one rather than many different entities with the same name. Entitypedia combines the richness of automatically assembled knowledge bases such as GeoNames and YAGO with the precision of a repository handcrafted by domain experts (see [1] [2] for a detailed discussion). All the steps described are reiterated whenever a user enters a new image, or a new source/media type is connected to the application.

Figure 3 shows a high level view of the CUBRIK pipeline described above, which consists of a sequence of both machine-executed tasks and human-executed tasks, with the goal of increasing the quality of the result with respect to fully automated solutions.

4.2   The Social Graph

Information on links between historical actors within CVCE's photo collection and other sources becomes visually accessible through the Social graph feature. The basis for the construction of any graph is the availability of structurally standardized dependencies between different types of entities that are to occur in the graph. These dependencies or links often vary in meaningfulness, the so-called link weight. The social graph in the History of Europe App aims at representing and visualizing dependencies between historically relevant persons in the context of European integration. Thereby the weight of the (social) links between person entities relies on their co-occurrence in historic photographs as identified by the aforementioned image indexation process. The more frequently two persons appear in different photographs, the stronger the link between the corresponding entities in the graph (see (2) for further details).

The resulting social graph is visualized by means of a force-directed graph layout that groups nodes with stronger link weights closer together than nodes with weaker links in such a way that a global optimum is reached. The visualization is performed by the javascript components Crossfilter and D3.js[9] that display the graph in the form of an interactive visual network of persons and connections between them. Thereby, each node represents a person and each edge represents the frequency of their co-occurrences in the given photo collection. The width of an edge represents the number of co-occurrences, in such way that a wider edge means that both persons appear simultaneously in a high number of photos (see figure 4 below).

Such network visualizations have the potential to highlight unexpected connections and patterns in all kinds of relations, be they between historical actors or other types of actors. In order to further evaluate any such finding it is however important to be able to interactively explore the relationships between the nodes, manipulate the parameters determining their visualization and re-contextualize the graph based on specific data subsets that are of interest to the user.

---

[8] see http://entitypedia.org/
[9] see http://d3js.org/

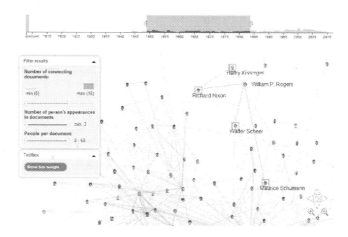

Fig. 4. Social Graph Overview

Users can interact with the History of Europe social graph in different ways. Since the documents stored in the collection very often come with a date of creation, the graph can be filtered by date with the timeline, displaying only the connections of documents created within this timespan. This timeline also shows the number of photos per date that are kept in the collection. Another filtering option is the number of connecting documents, which allows the visualization of those relationships that are only included in an interval of a minimum and maximum number of documents. This feature is useful to highlight highest co-occurrences. Finally, the number of appearances of a person in the processed collection lets us identify people who appear particularly often in any given time frame.

The photos used for the creation of the graph can be filtered according to the number of actors who were recognized in each photo. This filter is mainly used to show/hide those group pictures that include a high number of people on the same picture.

After selecting a person, the graph turns into an ego-graph (see figure 5), centering on the selected person and showing all relationships for the person. A click on an edge displays documents that relate to both selected relationship. All photos in which the selected person appears are displayed below the graph, sorted according to dates and in consideration of other filters. Users can review who is tagged in each of these photos by moving the mouse over them, which highlights the different persons that appear in the selected photo in the graph. In addition to these photos, a list of links to text documents that contain references to the selected person is displayed below the photos.

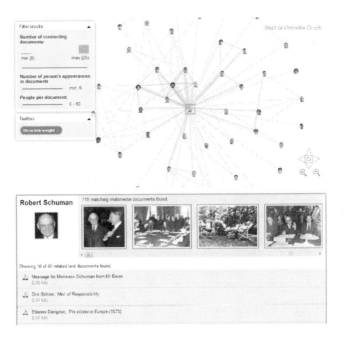

Fig. 5. Ego-Graph for Robert Schuman

Another powerful feature is the inspection of relationships. Whenever a user clicks on an edge between two persons, the selection shows all images and documents where both persons appear in and that therefore constitute the relationship between the persons.

4.3   Expert Sourcing and User Motivation

Crowdsourcing relies on the active contribution of a large number of persons. Existing platforms like Amazons Mechanical Turk[10] provide powerful incentive mechanisms (money) to source click-workers. Other approaches such as the Zooniverse[11] platform show, that sufficient numbers of volunteers exist who are willing to engage in crowdsourcing tasks in the natural sciences and humanities; and we plan to make use of it in the future development of the History of Europe app. These mechanisms however do not necessarily apply to the demands of expert users whose specific expertise is required in the validation of person identities and other information associated to historical documents. This chapter discusses the expert sourcing tasks in detail and develops an approach based on the results of the focus groups that were conducted with expert users at the CVCE. Furthermore we outline potential motivational factors and how they can be integrated in the interface. Finally we will discuss how different perspectives on a piece of information are integrated in

---

[10] https://www.mturk.com/mturk/welcome

[11] https://www.zooniverse.org

the interface of the app to stimulate discussions and preserve conflicting opinions beyond a binary concept of truth.

From Click-workers to Expert Sourcing

In the History of Europe application, two types of crowds are considered to solve different types of tasks driven by different types of motivation. On the one hand, click-workers are used to solve microtasks, i.e. small tasks which are easy to perform for most humans and which don't require domain knowledge. Click-workers can easily be motivated with e.g. monetary reward systems that pay workers per task. In the History of Europe application, click-workers contribute during the image indexation process by identifying and correcting false-positive and false-negative results of the face detection component via the external crowdsourcing platform "Microtask.com". However, when tasks get too complex and require more knowledge, click-workers often don't suffice. Harloff demonstrated in [3] that in the context of the History of Europe application, relying on click-workers for tasks such as the identification of persons in historic photos proves difficult: they are often of low resolution, taken from different viewpoints and depict the same persons in different historical periods. This makes face identification not only difficult for automatic methods but also for human users without appropriate background knowledge. For these kinds of tasks, a high level of domain knowledge is required which suggest the need to actively involve historians as a crowd of experts.

For the design of such expert-based crowdsourcing tasks, other types of motivational models apply. In order to motivate expert users to participate in improving the results of the automatic analysis and related tasks, the History of Europe application introduces a community-based exchange model. Mechanisms of community-based question-and-answer platforms such as Stackoverflow.com are explored, where users can build up social reputation within the community the more they contribute to answering requests of other users and be ranked according to their level of expertise (see [4],[5]). Collective action principles as they e.g. apply for Wikipedia [6], where users are also motivated by the notion of creating "public goods" by taking part in a process of collaborative knowledge building are also considered [7].

These mechanisms strongly influenced the design of the main functionalities of the History of Europe application that aim at involving and motivating a crowd of experts. As users of the application, historians can ask specific questions, i.e. initiate new research inquiries that are associated with multimedia content such as "Who is the person on the left?" (see Figure 6). They can then rely on a community of experts with a high level of domain knowledge, both within and beyond the application, to provide answers. For this, communication channels that are already being used by the historians to exchange knowledge, e.g. e-mail and the social media service Twitter will be integrated into the History of Europe application. Thus, research inquiries can still be distributed via established channels, but in a more structured way as before, making it easier for historians to get the information they need. Furthermore the results of this exchange are fed back into the system, thus allowing an improvement of the results of the automatic methods (e.g. by back propagation of the identified faces). This is a kind of explicit expert-based crowdsourcing approach.

Fig. 6. Research Inquiries (left) and media annotation tool considering multi-perspectivity (right) in the History of Europe application demo

At the same time, as part of their everyday research users can independently work on annotating the multimedia content of the application (see Figure 6). As the results are incorporated into the underlying knowledge base, the results of individual annotations are immediately visible and usable to others. This is an example of implicit expert-based crowdsourcing and collective action approach relying on the intrinsic motivation and reciprocal gratification of users.

In order for the application to be trustworthy and useful to historians in such a way that they would use it in a professional context, several challenges identified in focus groups needed to be overcome. The perceived authenticity of application by the users should be maximized, e.g. by linking users' identities from the History of Europe application to profiles from other professional networks or their official contact information. Provenance information of application content should be available and transparent. Another challenge relates to the traceability of annotations, which requires functionalities of enabling users to provide sources and explanations when making annotations. Results from automatic processes should also be as transparent as possible, not leaving any doubt of how they were calculated.

Expert User Motivation

Motivational aspects were explored both from the point of view of final users (having a request) and of the Expert Crowd (participating on request of a final user in the identification or enrichment of some multimedia content). Several methods (focus group, large-scale survey, interviews and user testing) were used to explore these motivations. In the case of the History of Europe application, on the one hand, final users' primary motivations for using the application were "competence" (enhancing one's skills and general knowledge in order to feel capable and effective in one's actions) and "autonomy" (possibility of achieving tasks autonomously and having different choices to achieve one's goal). On the other hand, results showed stimulation and relatedness as the main potential motivations of the crowd. The interface had therefore to be innovative enough to be felt as interesting and exciting.

Moreover, design elements able to support and highlight a relatedness experience (community aspects) were implemented within the application.

Modeling Opposing Perspectives on Truth

Another challenge for the HoE app and the domain of the Digital Humanities in general is the conception of truth, which differs significantly e.g. to the conceptions of truth in Computer Science. Computer Scientists can rely on a stable foundation of what is true: Any experiment can be replicated and measured precisely. In the humanities the concept of truth is far more complex: It is based on the insight, that there is no neutral or objective way to study human environments. The way, in which questions are asked, how data is selected to answer them, by what means this data is analyzed and finally the way in which the results of such analyses are communicated and received all challenge the idea of "one truth". Consider the common saying "One man's terrorist is another's freedom fighter": Any such attribution inherently depends on individual viewpoints, experiences and socializations. It becomes apparent, that the interpretation and communication of historical events is directly linked to our perspective on the past as a whole. Having made this point, it is not hard to imagine how difficult it is to identify causal factors in historical events.

The negotiation of and reasoning behind these problems are of direct relevance for the design of the History of Europe application. While there might be less conflict when it comes to associating names and faces on photographs, it is more likely that the meaning attributed to a certain photo is challenged. Just like the verbs discussed in the previous paragraph. Similarly to words, images bring with them their own "spin" on events which depend on composition, postures, gestures, angle and so on.

For these reasons, humanities scholars need the freedom to discuss competing interpretations and to see historical events and sources in the light of different research interests. In the context of the History of Europe application, scholars therefore have the opportunity to add more than one annotation, e.g. different captions to a photograph, and to comment on others, enabling academic discussion and competing interpretations. Users can vote annotations up and down, thereby relying on the wisdom of the expert crowd to identify the best annotation without simply overwriting less popular answers (see Figure 6). All these elements remain open for improvement and editing, thereby keeping the system flexible and responsive for new information.

5   Conclusion and Future Work

The History of Europe application takes on the challenge to combine cutting edge research in the domains of computer science, the design of human-computation tasks, data visualization, social engineering and the humanities by identifying synergies between the disciplines' strengths and by compensating for their weaknesses. We do this by building a pipeline which connects face recognition tools, data visualization and input from humans and creates an ongoing cycle of iteratively improved user input and machine output.

The History of Europe application stands in line with a range of other online tools for historical research[12] but introduces new social features as well as crowdsourcing from both click-workers and expert users, which continuously improves the system. In contrast to other approaches, the History of Europe application does not operate with an inflexible understanding of truth: it uses the wisdom of a crowd of experts to give input and evaluate it by relying on a robust system of discussion.

In this early phase, the demo application is built for the analysis of more than 3000 photographs that chronicle the History of European Integration. In the future we will expand the selection of sources to include large collections of digitized photographs, text documents as well as audio material and video interviews from different archives.

References

1. Giunchiglia, F., Maltese, V., Dutta, B.: Domains and context: First steps towards managing diversity in knowledge. J. Web Sem. 12, 53–63 (2012)
2. Dioniso, M., Fraternali, P., Martinenghi, D., Pasini, C., Tagliasacchi, M., Harlof, E., et al.: Building social graphs from images through expert-based crowdsourcing. In: Proceedings of the International Workshop on Social Media for Crowdsourcing and Human Computation, Paris (2013)
3. Harloff, E.: Who is this person? Konzeption und prototypische Evaluierung einer Crowdsourcing-Anwendung für Multimedia-Suche. Fachhochschule Stralsund, Fachbereich Wirtschaft (2012)
4. Preece, J.: Online Communities: Designing Usability and Supporting Socialbilty, 1st edn. John Wiley & Sons, Inc., New York (2000)
5. Tedjamulia, S.J.J., Dean, D.L., Olsen, D.R., Albrecht, C.C.: Motivating Content Contributions to Online Communities: Toward a More Comprehensive Theory. In: Proceedings of the 38th Annual Hawaii International Conference on System Sciences, HICSS 2005, p. 193b (2005)
6. Nov, O.: What motivates Wikipedians? Commun. ACM 50(11), 60–64 (2007)
7. Marwell, G., Oliver, P.: The Critical Mass in Collective Action. Cambridge University Press (1993)

---

[12] See for example: ePistolarium (http://ckcc.huygens.knaw.nl/epistolarium), Pelagios (http://pelagios-project.blogspot.de/), the Republic of Letters (http://republicofletters.stanford.edu/) or The Proceedings of the Old Bailey (http://www.oldbaileyonline.org /)

From Diagram to Network

A Multi-mode Network Approach to Analyze Diagrams of Art History

Yanan Sun

Cornell University, Ithaca, USA
ys479@cornell.edu

Abstract. This paper aims to remove a constraint of applying network approach to art history. First, it points out, although old diagrams of art history did not use the language of modern network theory, they have already shown ingenuous network thinking to theorize the development of arts. Meanwhile, the indirect visual devices and the embracive tradition of these diagrams, which includes entities in various properties, prevent the application of computer-aided network methods to decipher and re-analyze the contents of this heritage of art historical research. To break this shackle, this paper suggests a multi-mode network approach to "translate" the traditional network thinking of art diagrams to the conceptualization of graph-theoretical network analysis. By doing so, this paper demonstrates how art historical research could benefit from modern sociological approach to network theory. To explain the usefulness and advantage of this method, the diagrams of Covarrubias and Barr are taken as examples to be converted into graph-theoretical networks.

Keywords: multi-mode network, historic network research, art history, art-history diagram.

1 Introduction

Previous studies in digital humanities[1] have repeatedly demonstrated the advantage of network methods in inventorying, visualizing, and quickly extracting information from a large number of historical resources in the field of art history. However, before these contemporary applications, network thinking was not completely strange in art history. At the beginning of the last century, diagrams outlining linkage among entities, e.g., artists, art styles, artworks, provided an alternative perspective to analyze and visualize the development of arts. Many of these diagrams have become valuable historical records themselves as witness of the development of art theory in the past.

Meanwhile, art history still dwells in the early stages of exploring how network method can transform its scholarship. Not surprisingly, a number of constraints still

---

[1] For example, the projects of London Exhibition and Van Gogh Museum, see [1, 2].

A. Nadamoto et al. (Eds.): SocInfo 2013 Workshops, LNCS 8359, pp. 100–109, 2014.

fetter its application in the field, one of which is how to embrace the great variety of entities that are traditionally included in art historiography. How to deal with the relations that are disguised in indirect visual forms in order to interpret and re-present the budding network thinking? This paper offers a solution from the approach of the multi-modal network. To explain how to apply this method, two diagrams, Corarrubias' and Barr's charts, are transformed into networks in the manner of graph theory, which enables us to analyze them with graph-mathematical methods.

2   Diagrams of Art History

2.1   Diagrams: Heritage of Art Historical Research

Thinking diagrammatically as a way of conceptualizing our world has been in existence from the moment the first cave-person picked up a soft "rock" and started making markings on the walls of his/her dwelling [7]. As civilization progresses, this visual device has established itself as an important carrier of the intellectual legacy of the mankind[2]. The diagrams of art history are no exception. Diagrams, illustrating the arguments, assumptions, speculations, conceptualizations, and conclusions of historians, are undisputable heritage of the discipline. Although diagrams were usually produced only in limited number of copies, they contain a large amount of wisdom in the past. To understand this historical heritage, it is imperative to digitalize them in a manner that contents can also be investigated with modern methodology.

2.2   Diagrams : Nascent Network Thinking in Art History

Traditionally, study of art history is a long procedure of information collection and synthesis, which results in the multifariousness of evidence to support arguments. To outline the development path of artistic styles, diagrams were employed, which, thanks to their structuralist preference, discloses a kind of nascent network thinking in art history. By showing emphasis on connections, they present the growth of arts as being entwined in a mesh of entities. However, this network thinking is in many aspects different from contemporary network analysis that is built on graph theory. Art diagrams are theory-driven, i.e., they visualize art historians' conceptualization of a knowledge space. The current network method, in contrast, produces emergent results according to some proper algorithm. Moreover, being designed in artistic forms, art-historical diagrams do not usually have a straightforward graph of "dots and lines." Equipped with all kinds of visual devices, the connections in art diagrams are loosely defined, whose meanings vary constantly to cater the need of historians' theorization.

On the other hand, this liberty of composition avails the authors to include more types of entities. Free from any technical constraints, they display the natural thinking model of historiographic research, in which artists, art works, locations, as well as sources and inspirations are all considered. The theorization of multi-complex relations among these entities is the main scholarly contribution of art-historical diagrams to the field.

---

[2] More about the relation between knowledge and diagram, see [3 - 6].

2.3   Diagrams of Covarrubias and Barr

Linking lines, arrows, and influence trees in traditional art diagrams bring with them many implicit but powerful assumptions based on "influence relation [8]," which is equally true to the charts of Corarrubias and Barr. Having no intention of inviting us to pay close attention to individual artists and their interpersonal relations, these diagrams aim to provide a understanding of entirety, i.e., the abstract concepts and theories that have been formed by historians before drawing them into illustrations.

Covarrubias 1933. *The Tree of Modern Art—Planted 60 Years Ago* - by Miguel Covarrubias in 1933 is one of the earliest diagrams for modern arts. Although the illustration is not in a dot-and-line form, the connections are easy to see, as being helped by the common sense in the growth of a tree. Leaves of the tree are artists, while roots, trunks and branches are alternatively artists or art schools. The trunk splits into different limbs, assuming the later styles "grow" out of the earlier "impressionists (fig.1)."

Barr Chart 1936. An earnest follower of Covarrubias is Alfred Barr, who produced a diagram for the Museum of Modern Art (MoMA) in 1936, as an important visual summary of artistic kinship somewhere else in his essay. Barr charts art movements more than individual artists, and naturally he dispenses with the niceties of a "tree" in favor of a flowchart [9] (fig.3).

3   Multi-mode Network Approach

3.1   Some Basics of Social Network Analysis

Social Network Analysis (SNA) is the method that studies social relations with network theory by taking the prepositions of graph theory and applies them to social world. In its basic form, a social network is a network consists of nodes, representing actors, and ties, representing a form of social relationship such as friendship. SNA uses sociometric to note pairwise relations, which is indexed by the set of originating actors (for its rows) and the set of receiving actors (for its columns) and gives the values of the ties from the row actors to the column actors [10]. In its graphic form, actors are represented as nodes, while lines symbolize relations among them.

Based on nodes and ties, the field of SNA has developed a large body of terminology. Particularly relevant to this research is the concept of "mode," which is a class of nodes of some common properties. For instance, a mode of human beings may have different persons, e.g., Michael and John, while a mode of locations may have cities of London and Paris. Traditionally, SNA focuses mainly on single or at most two-mode data and considers only one type of ties at a time [10], which increasingly constraints research that intends to study more complex social problems.

3.2   Multi-mode Approach

The increasing quantity of data and the success of applying network approach in other historical fields tantalize art historians to experiment this method as well. Some scholars have already led the way to study art history with graph-theoretical network methods. The diagram for Abstraction in MoMA [14] and Helmreich's study on art market in London [15] are representative examples to demonstrate how art history research could benefit from analytical tools in sociology. Both projects root their statements in the algorithmic analysis of the network, while historiographic approach recedes from the dictatorial position. Compared with art-historical diagrams, pioneer projects seem to have restrained research scopes, thereby eschewing the multi-modality of entities.

Fig. 1. The Tree of Modern Art, Covarrubias 1933, source: [6]

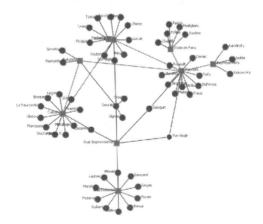

Fig. 2. Graph-theoretical network of Covarrubias' tree

When resorting to graph theory to examine the network ideas in art-historical diagrams, their nature of multi-modality should be first recognized, in order to understand the comprehensive tradition of historiography. Given the definition of "mode" in graph theory, multi-mode refers to network that has more than two classes of nodes. Besides modes of human beings, multi-mode network also allows us to create non-human modes, such as locations and art works.

The key step of converting historiographic diagrams to multi-mode network is to differentiate who (e.g., artists, and buyers in MoMA's and Helmreich's projects), what (e.g. paintings, sculptures, architecture), where (e.g., Paris, London, New York), and when. With further expansion, such as education and financial resources, we may even explain why and how. To find the inter-relationship that is intended by the drawers, the "cosmetic veneer" needs to be peeled off to expose the essential structure of the network thinking in these diagrams. For instance, the connections between trunk and branches in the tree form are going to be recognized as influential relations that are insinuated by the author.

Notice we should always be aware of the different nature of links between human entities and nonhuman entities. Although some scholars hold, tools of network analysis are based on the mathematics of graph theory, therefore applicable regardless of the type of nodes or the reason for the connections [13], I am reluctant to agree. We should always be aware, in multi-mode networks, many nodes do not have social features. For instance, technically, nodes of two buildings can be lined up, using the argument that they share common architectural features. But a building cannot "interact" with another in the way as an architect with another. Thus, many algorithmic measures such as authority and diffusion thresholds, which are dedicated to human relations, need sound justifications before being applied to nonhuman relations.

4   Convert Art-Historical Diagrams to Graph-Theoretical Networks

Previous studies have shown how to use multi-mode method to build network from textual documents [14, 15]. Here, its application is extended to graphic documents. By building graph-theoretical networks from Covarrubias' and Barr's diagrams, I also distinguish historical network research from network methods used in "text-mining," which touches little upon nontextual resources of history. It is especially eye-opening to compare the results after the conversion, because both diagrams deal with the same period of modern arts, i.e., 1890 - 1930.

4.1   Detect Actors and Relations in Covarrubias' and Barr's Diagrams

The diagram of Covarrubias mainly answers one question: Which styles that contain which artists, influence which later styles? In the upper part of the diagram, i.e., above the root, two node classes can be defined: style and artist. Our common sense about

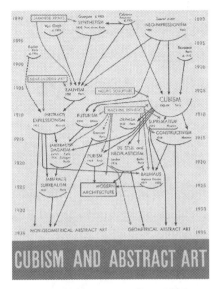

Fig. 3. Cubism and Abstract art, Barr, 1936, source: [8]

trees helps to define two types of relations, (1) the sequential influence between art schools as being indicated by connections of trunk and branches, (2) the affiliation of artists to certain art school as being suggested by the arrangement that leaves grow out of a certain branch. Accordingly, two matrices can be built, Styles x Styles and Artists x Styles.

One exception occurs by Seurat, whose branch does not have a name for the style,[3] thereby giving a unique connection, artist influences style,[3] which raises the question of ontological unification. Similar to the pre-process of "machine teaching" in text mining in order to refine and make sense of raw records, network building also needs pre-process which involves, most importantly, unifying node titles, links, and matrices ontologically. This technique will be applied later in this research, when networks of the two diagrams are compared and contrasted.

In the lower part, i.e., below the soil line, while it is clear that root branches indicate their "influential nutrition" to the trunk of "Impressionists," it is difficult to integrate the objects, e.g., Negro sculpture, which scatter around, into the system of the tree. As intended by the design device, they are not supposed to be included into the arborization on which they cast influence. This treatment is not consistent with the network thinking of the upper part, therefore will not be converted.

In comparison, Barr's chart, though deals with the same period of art, contains a greater diversity of entities, viz., art styles/schools, year[4], artists, locations and

---

[3] This means, we have two matrices of Artists x Styles, i.e., two different kinds of relations between these two node classes of artists and styles. In graph theory, it is normal to have more than one type of relations between the same two classes of nodes.

[4] The inclusion of chronological information belongs to the field of dynamic network analysis. For the limitation of length, this paper does not address this issue, and assumes the diagrams present the accumulation of artistic influence at an ending point of time.

inspirations. The diagram seems to answer the same question of Covarrubias' tree, while providing more information such as where, with what reference. Therefore, besides modes of artists and art schools, this chart has two more modes – inspiration and location. While arrowed lines indicate the influence among styles and inspirations, the spatial arrangement of clumps shows the affiliation of artists to certain styles and the location of a style to certain cities.

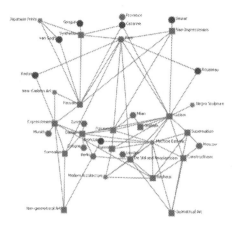

Fig. 4. Graph-theoretical network of Barr's chart

Based on the above analysis, networks can be built for both diagrams, which shows similarities as well as distinguishes of the understanding of the development of modern arts between the two authors. While Covarrubias focuses on individual artist, Barr intends to show a broader historical sphere that incubated the development of abstract art (fig.2, fig.4, produced by software ORA).

4.2   Form: Tree Form versus Flow Chart

While Covarrubias uses branching to express the relationship among styles, Barr chooses arrow lines of flow. The tree form is relatively intuitive to readers and can suggest a temporal sequence without giving exactly information of years. However, this form limits the expression of network thinking in the sense that no more objects other than "leaves" and "trunk and branches" can be added to give more information. Covarrubias may have equally felt the importance of other entities, such as Negro sculpture, but could only place them out of the tree system. Moreover, the fact that tree can only branch off but not re-grow together prevents the expression of influence from more than one earlier sources. While Barr drew an arrow between Futurism and Dadaism, they are only two offshoots respectively from Cubism and Surrealism in the tree of Covarrubias. In fact, even if Covarrubias had recognized the influence between Futurism and Dadaism, the natural form of a tree would not provide a possibility to connect them. At where the branches of Fauvism and Cubism join into Surrealism, he actually artificially, forcibly knots the branches together. To convert this part, one can only draw on the faint silhouette of the brushwork and educated speculations. In comparison, flow chart is free from these design restrictions and can draw connections between any two entities. Most importantly, flow chart can integrate all entities into its network thinking, therefore can be without information loss converted into modern networks. However, flow chart needs "a side bar" to indicate time sequence; it is less intuitively "theory – exhibiting," therefore, more abstract than tree form.

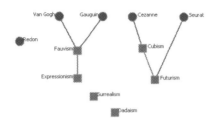

Fig. 5. Common features in the two diagrams

4.3   Compare the Theorization of Covarrubias and Barr

To compare the conceptualization of the two diagrams, graph mathematics can be of great help. First, by intersecting the two networks with each other, the features that are shared by both diagrams become immediately apparent. Figure 5 shows styles of Fauvism, Cubism, Futurism, Expressionism, Dadaism, and Surrealism, artists of Cezanne, Gauguin, Van Gogh, Seurat, and Redon are common in both diagrams, implying both graphs agree that Cezanne, Gauguin, Van Gogh, and Seurat were the founding figures in modern arts and that the development of modern arts were centered on the above mentioned styles. About how these styles influence each other in the later period, however, the two graphs do not consist with each other completely.

To clarify the difference between the theorization of the two diagrams about how the modern art develops among the recognized styles and artists, we strip off the nodes that are not shown in the result of intersection, keep only common nodes in the original networks, which results in two sub-networks. For the purpose of ontological unification, the nodes of Synthetism and Neo-Impressionism are equalized with Gauguin and Seurat in the network of Barr Chart. That is, the styles of Synthetism and Neo-Impressionism in Barr's chart are replaced respectively by Gauguin and Seurat, because in the tree graph, the names of the artists are used as embodiment of their styles.

By overlaying these two sub-networks (fig. 6), it becomes clear how the conceptualization of the two diagrams differentiate with each other.

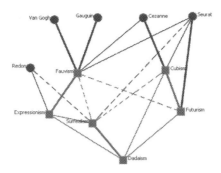

Fig. 6. Difference in theorization of the development of modern arts between Covarrubias and Barr (Thicker lines indicate connections appear in both diagrams; dash lines signify the connections only appear in Covarrubias' tree, while thin solid lines mean connections that are only shown in Barr's chart.)

5   Advantages of Multi-mode Network Approach

There are three major advantages of adopting multi-mode network approach to examine diagrams of art history.

First, multi-mode approach allows art historians to include both human and nonhuman entities into their analysis. In historiography, scholars can synthesize contents of all resources in a black box, i.e., the smart brain; such highly intellectual process, however, cannot be directly copied to machine. Constraints and rules have to be followed to digitally use the resources that we have. While one-mode network approach uses only part of the resources in stock, multi-mode approach helps us to include more. This is especially crucial to art history, for nonhuman entities, such as artistic works, are major evidence to ground arguments.

Second, the examples in this paper show multi-mode approach can be equally useful to digitalize non-textual documents. In historioinformatics, while "machine reading" for textual materials is well-developed, other forms of historical sources, such as architectural drawings and artifacts, still need "human reading." To digitalize the contents of human reading, a structuralized conceptualization is demanded. Beyond methods such as machine training or meta-data, multi-mode network provides an approach that is amiable to art historians.

Third, this paper shows it is possible to compare contents of non-textual sources straightforwardly, when artistic device are removed while information is preserved in entirety. This means, besides bringing the past intellectual treasure of art history into the era of digital humanities, multi-mode network also sets the accurateness of information free from constraints of old visual forms.

6   Conclusion

Network thinking is not completely new in the field of art history. However, its tradition of synthesizing all types of entities in all forms of visual embodiments is greatly challenged by technical requirements of graph-theoretical network methods. This paper proposes multi-mode network method can provide not only a solution to resolve this challenge, but also a potential, overarching methodology to inventory and analyze graphic sources of history.

References

1. University of Glasgow: Exhibition Culture in London 1878-1908 (2006), http://www.exhibitionculture.arts.gla.ac.uk/
2. Van Gogh Museum: Vincent Van Gogh - The Letters (2012), http://vangoghletters.org/vg/
3. Mitchell, W.J.T.: Picture theory. [Essays on verbal and visual representation]. Univ. of Chicago Press, Chicago (1995)
4. Boehm, G.: Die Wiederkehr der Bilder. In: Boehm, G. (ed.) Was ist ein Bild? Bild und Text, 2nd edn., pp. 11–38. W. Fink, München (1995, c1994)
5. Ong, W.J.: From allegory to diagram in the renaissance mind. A Study in the Significance of the Allegorical Tableau. s.n., S.l. (1959)
6. Bruno, G., Higgins, D.: On the composition of images, signs & ideas. Willis, Locker & Owens, New York (1991)
7. Lee, C.A.L.: The Science and Art of the Diagrams. Culturing Physics and Mathematics (2013), http://blogs.scientificamerican.com/guest-blog/2013/03/22/the-science-and-art-of-the-diagrams-culturing-physics-and-mathematics-part-i/
8. Tufte, E.: Design of causal diagrams. Barr art chart, Lombardi diagrams, evolutionary trees, Feynman diagrams, timelines, http://www.edwardtufte.com/bboard/q-and-a-fetch-msg?msg_id=0000yO
9. Poundstone, W.: The Tree of Art (2012), http://blogs.artinfo.com/lacmonfire/2012/02/13/the-tree-of-art/
10. Wasserman, S., Faust, K.: Social Network Analysis: Methods and Applications. In: Structural Analysis in the Social Sciences, vol. 8. Cambridge University Press, New York (1994)
11. Exhibition's curatorial and design team, Ingram, P., Banerjee, M.: Diagram for Inventing Abstraction (2013), http://www.moma.org/interactives/exhibitions/2012/inventingabstraction/?page=connections
12. Helmreich, A.: The Global. Goupil & Cie/Boussod, Valadon & Cie and International Networks. Nineteenth-Century Art Worldwide 11(3) (2012)
13. Carley, K.M., Pfeffer, J., Reminga, J., Storrick, J., Columbus, D.: ORA User's Guide 2013 (2013), http://www.casos.cs.cmu.edu/publications/papers/CMU-ISR-13-108.pdf
14. Carley, K.M.: Toward an interoperable dynamic network analysis toolkit. Decision Support Systems 43(4), 1324–1347 (2007)
15. Diesner, J.: Conditional random fields for entity extraction and ontological text coding. Computational & Mathematical Organization Theory 14(3), 248–262 (2008)

Frame-Based Models of Communities and Their History

Robert B. Allen

Research Center for Knowledge Communities, University of Tsukuba, Japan
rba@boballen.info

Abstract. Previous models of communities and their history have focused on the entities in those communities such as their locations and people. We introduce models which incorporate behaviors and processes. We propose that approaches based on object-oriented modeling are particularly useful. Specifically, we explore the feasibility of developing object-oriented models which employ linguistic frames adapted from the FrameNet corpus. We apply these models to relatively straightforward and self-contained historical scenarios. We implement the models in Java and analyze some of advantages and challenges in that approach. Historical newspapers are particularly rich sources of natural language descriptions about communities but there are many sources of non-linguistic information about communities which may also be incorporated. We consider the possibilities of developing more coherent models of communities based on modeling processes, partonomies, systems, and situations. Finally, we consider enabling greater interactivity with the structured models and alternative architectures for the models.

Keywords: Behavior, Descriptive Modeling, Digital Humanities, Events, Functionality, FrameNet, Indexing, Information Organization, Java, Object-Oriented Modeling, Processes, Social Modeling.

1 Modeling History and Communities

History has rich sources of evidence but they are challenging to organize and access. In an approach we describe as model-oriented information organization, we propose that explicit behavior-based modeling could improve indexing and be more effective than traditional descriptions of historical documents, artifacts, or communities. Systematic models used in software engineering are particularly appealing because many tools have been developed to implement and interact with them.

We focus on modeling communities because they are relatively self-contained. Even a relatively small town will have hundreds of residents and each of them is involved in myriad activities. Moreover, modeling history meaningfully requires a great amount of detail and the specification of a great deal of context. Fortunately, digitized historical newspapers and other historical records contain a vast amount of detailed information relating to communities.

Some of our earlier work explored supporting access to massive collections of digitized historical newspapers and the challenge of organizing that newspaper content. Because there are few standardized structures in historical newspapers, it is difficult even to consistently identify newspaper articles, let alone index them. As an

A. Nadamoto et al. (Eds.): SocInfo 2013 Workshops, LNCS 8359, pp. 110–119, 2014.
© Springer-Verlag Berlin Heidelberg 2014

alternative to applying simple metadata labels for the articles, we propose organizing the material by developing models of the content [1, 8].

Explicit modeling could support access by improving the accuracy of human retrieval from historical newspapers and in turn greater accuracy should drive refinement of the models. Similarly, the models can improve the accuracy of the text extraction and, in turn, text extraction can populate the models.

There are different levels of detail and coherence in community models. We developed a prototype interactive directory of the entities in a Midwestern US town for 1899 to 1900 [6]. That directory combines data about people, businesses, and locations obtained from census records, historical city directories, and digitized historical newspapers. However, the interactive directory does not describe either typical processes or the details of specific events. Here we explore implementing a richer community model which includes behaviors specified with Java classes based on text descriptions. We also provide a conceptual framework and some additional world knowledge for structuring models of the entities and events related to the community.

2   Entities, Frames, and World Knowledge

Frames are flexible structures employed in artificial intelligence and software engineering for describing complex objects. While the entities we describe are often far more complex than those in most software engineering applications, frames offer a fruitful approach to describing them. For modeling textual descriptions we employ FrameNet [10, 12] which uses frames to capture concepts expressed in natural language. FrameNet was based on a cognitive model in which the linguistic frames were determined by typical usage. We use the collection of frames as a resource for information organization. Importantly, FrameNet includes frames for verbs. These describe how the frame values are changed as a result of an event [2, 8].

We modeled the attributes of individuals and organizations. Our entities are often variations of common structures; people have predictable biological structures and somewhat more variable, but still often predictable, social structures. We combined entities with a conceptual model knowledgebase and world knowledge beyond what was in the newspapers we sampled. The knowledgebase classified entities and facilitated inheritance. The world knowledge included both details about instances (e.g., street names, the names of businesses, the names and roles of government officials (cf. [3]), and the names of children in the 4th grade class in the local school), and about processes (e.g., local laws, rituals, train schedules, etc.). Some of the world knowledge overlaps with the information in an interactive city directory [6].

We focus on description rather than inference, because of the complexity of making automated inferences. We allow low-level inferences for actions which are implied but omitted in written language, but we particularly avoid automated inferences about motives, trends, or theories because of the difficulties of large scale AI systems in doing so, rather we emphasize successful large-scale descriptive systems such as UMLS.

3   Frame-like Models with Java

Many software and knowledge engineering tools have been developed to model specific activities in communities, modeling a limited aspect of the entire community. For greater robustness and support, we adopted a general-purpose programming language and coded the natural-language-like structures needed. We selected an object-oriented programming language so that we could also model the behavior of entities and relationships with other entities. We adopted Java. Because sequences of events unfold across time, we allow the representation to unfold. That is, we run the model to determine the states rather than try to statically spatialize the context for each event.

Natural language is the basis of the modeling in this paper, in that we apply limited preprocessing of texts to show a coherent set of actions. In doing so, we remain as close to the source text as possible so as to remain as faithful to the history (as it was written) as possible. It is useful to think of many concepts as inheriting attributes and behaviors from broader classes. A person is a physical object with mass and shape as well as an animal which breaths, moves, and eats. Similarly, the shops in the community such as the bakery and dry goods shop share attributes as retail businesses. We defined entity classes for geographic features, governmental units, businesses, and individuals. Once the classes were defined, we instantiated specific entities. Those instantiated entities were recorded in an EntityLog array (Fig. 1).

```
// main:
    entityLog[entityLogCnt] = new EntityLog();
    entityLog[entityLogCnt].typeCnt=person_cnt;
    entityLog[entityLogCnt].type="Person";
    entityLog[entityLogCnt].instanceName="FatherHennipin";
    entityLogcnt++;
```

Fig. 1. Entry in the EntityLog to record that a Person entity has been instantiated. There is a similar log for events.

Verb frames were implemented as Java classes with methods. A specific event was described by instantiating the verb frame class and passing entities to it as arguments. As a result of the methods, the values of one or more entity attributes are changed (cf., [2]). Fig. 2, shows a Java class implementation of the verb frame for releasing a captive. In this case, the state of a variable indicating whether the captive person is a prisoner is set to *false*. We recognize this is a simplistic quasi-attribute and we discuss alternatives in [7].

```
class V_Release {
    public V_Release(Person Captor, Person Captive){
        Captive.isPrisoner=false;}
```

Fig. 2. Java class for "release" frame

4   Some Solutions and Some Challenges

4.1   Sample Encoded Text Passage

We focused on encyclopedia-level descriptions because they generally use straightforward language with relatively little metaphor. Such texts still include unstated gaps and assumptions (see [7]) but these seemed fairly uncontroversial and we used our best judgment in coding them. As an example text, we selected a passage from Wikipedia about the early history of Minneapolis, Minnesota.[1] We instantiated Person entities for the explorers Daniel Greysolon, Father Hennipin, and two unnamed individuals. [2] Hennipin and the unnamed individuals formed an AdHocGroup which had been captured and was being held by the Dakota Tribe. The Dakotas were instantiated as a FormalGroup. In a sequence of events described in the Wikipedia entry Greysolon requested the Dakotas to release Hennipin and the others. After being released, Hennipin "discovers" and names St. Anthony Falls. A later segment of the Wikipedia passage briefly describes the development of the area around the Falls into a mill district.

4.2   Model Elements: Partonomies, Processes, and Systems

Because the entities we consider are highly complex and because they often interact in predictable ways we develop model elements. The entities complex entities can be separated into parts and can be described with partonomies. Geographic locations are parts of other locations. As noted in the previous section, many activities involve either ad hoc groups or formal groups. Grouping is a partonomic relationship [14]. For AdHocGroups, we developed a transient entity which contains an array of instances. FormalGroups also have an array of members but the group is also a formal entity in itself and has its own attributes.

Many events are part of an established sequence and that sequence itself can be treated as an entity. In earlier work, we suggested that predefined or expected sequences could be modeled with processes. Several types of processes can be distinguished. A process may simply iterate through an ordered list. Or, there may be Petri-Net-like sequences in which the order can be relatively unimportant. Moreover, these processes may be enhanced with constraints on the entities involved. For instance, a Recipe specifies both quantities and qualities of each of its ingredients (e.g., "take two large eggs").

Systems and Situations combine entities and processes. The entities are often partonomic and a system may itself be an entity in which the processes describing the relationship of the parts. Systems include organizations and machines but they can also include static relationships such as the walls of a house holding up the roof. A Situation is an interaction of specific entities and it may be either in stasis or evolving.

---

[1] http://en.wikipedia.org/wiki/History_of_Minneapolis retrieved on August 3, 2013.

[2] Recently, the text of the Wikipedia entry has been modified to include the names of the un-named individuals.

We found it difficult to distinguish between classes and instances for complex entities. For instance, a given house may be an instance of the house class but instantiation of the high-level class does not specify all the details of that house (e.g., whether it has a separate dining room). We may need multi-leveled inheritance for complex object concepts and instances of those objects. Moreover, the typical parts of complex entities may change and considerable care is needed to distinguish between changes in the relationship of classes (the information structure) and changes in the instances.

4.3   Capturing the Nuance and Ambiguity of Natural Language

Language is highly nuanced. Consider the relationship of Baker, Bakery, and BakedGoods. The pattern of Occupation, Shop, and Product of Occupation is mirrored by Pharmacist, Pharmacy, and Pharmaceuticals and by Printer, PrintShop, and PrintedMaterials. However, it breaks down in other cases such as Librarian and Library where a service is provided rather than a product. The distinction between product-oriented organizations and service-oriented organizations is well understood in economics but those concepts have not been integrated with an overarching framework for communities.

There are nuances in the usage of even a relatively simple term such as Baking. "To bake" may mean simply to heat to a high temperature, may refer to a particular phase of cooking, or may mean the preparation of an entire food item (e.g., "he baked some bread"). The simplest word sense of baking involves one state change. More complex forms are a sequence of actions which include the simple action of baking. This extension of a simple action into a flow of actions is related to but richer than the inheritance of the method because the embedded action is integrated with the other actions. Likewise, a Baker could be someone who bakes a single item or it could be a person who has the occupation of Baking; further that occupation is associated with many other concepts.

As another example of complexity in language, consider that a Library is often, but not always, a CulturalInstitution. Indeed, an entity may change classifications and we need to be able to describe it during the transition when it may have mixed attributes. For instance, a Library may initially belong to a group or individual and later be opened as a public CulturalInstitution.

Verbs will apply across entire classes of entities which may not be congruent with the established class hierarchies. In the example passage, for instance, a Person (Greysolon) made a request of the Formal Group (the Dakota Tribe). A request can be made by any Agent to any other Agent whether a Person or a Formal Group. However, because Person is part of the sentient organism hierarchy we cannot also make it part of an Agent hierarchy which includes Groups. We considered overloading constructors but using Java Implements for an Interface was simpler. Still, there are additional cases where a more flexible approach is needed. A Baker may have several different roles. The Baker may also be the Manager and the Owner of the Bakery. While multiple inheritance is generally discouraged in object-oriented design with languages such as Java, it seems difficult to avoid when the goal is modeling natural language usage.

Ultimately, we need standards to encourage consistency and a flexible modeling structure. Beyond nuance, natural language is also ambiguous. Even in textbook-level histories, there is considerable ambiguity. For instance, in reading the passage about Greysolon we assume that the Dakotas granted Greysolon's request to release Hennipin (rather than, say, Hennipin escaping) but that is not stated specifically. Such low-level inferences are largely uncontroversial and are accepted by most readers but should be noted.

There are also challenges in modeling generalizations. While we may know that most 10 year old American children spend their days at school it is obviously not always the case that a given child will be in school on a given day. We can state it as a generally true statement and as an expectation but, ideally, we would also identify the situations when it might not hold.

5   Broad Issues and Next Steps

A brief passage has been coded and the models we have implemented thus far are fairly basic. We need to expand the coverage and address more complex passages. Here, we consider some broader issues.

5.1   Modeling People: Mental Events, Knowledge, and Intentions

The entities describing People and Organizations are the most complex entity types in this implementation. Other parameters may have been described simplistically. For instance, when Father Hennipin was captured we noted his being held as change of state. But, should we have a separate state associated with every different verb? In [7] we suggest the need to explicitly model Situations. Some of the states of a person could be determined by the reference to the Situations they encounter.

Following the distinction made in [4, 5], in this initial study we focused on observable entities and events. Thus, we have excluded consideration of mental events and explanations including descriptions of people's reasoning. However, many explanations are based on attributions to a person's mental state. The attribution of mental events is so common for causal explanations that we need general strategies for modeling them. In any event, to the extent that we capture the gist of the words used to describe the mental states and the explanations based on descriptions of the mental states, we should be able to model them without being able to make generalizations.

Mental states which include beliefs, knowledge, and intentions are common in mental events such as inferences and decision making. Presumably a Baker both does the action of Baking and has knowledge of how to bake. But, it is unclear exactly what specific skills should be enumerated to cover knowledge of baking, let alone more complex skills such as knowledge of singing or of a foreign language. We may more readily represent abstractions which could include likely behaviors associated with having a given skill, instead of representing each person's knowledge in detail. For instance, knowledge of a foreign language is reflected in a person's ability to communicate in a country where that is the local language. Groups such as organizations, institutions and communities present analogous challenges. Groups have expectations, norms and knowledge. The challenge of representing these parameters is increased by the fact that groups may lack a consensus among their members on them.

Furthermore, human language users have widely differing understandings of concepts such as knowledge and norms. It remains an open question about the extent to which an information organization system should try to replicate mental models of individual human language users. In many cases, it may be better for the information organization system to approximate a typical language user. Essentially, the question is the extent to which the system should model a knowledgeable person or should it attempt to model every possible detail about every known entity and event. We need flexible multi-level representation management systems.

5.2   Object Instance Metadata and Other Annotations

While in the present study all of the text comes from one source, we envision weaving together text from multiple sources. Ideally, the source of all claims would be documented. Potentially, parallel versions of history could be woven together, especially if the versions were consistent. For instance, a user could decide whether to browse a simple biography of Daniel Greysolon or a more detailed one. If the descriptions are inconsistent, version management will be needed.

5.3   Explanations, Narrative, and Argumentation

As suggested by [5] discourse structures such as for narrative, explanation, and argumentation may be added over the base entity-event fabric. We noted the potential for narrative earlier in this paper. Explanations are often based on mental events (Section 5.1) to account for a person's actions. Argumentation may evaluate evidence or contrast explanations. Additional rhetorical structures may be defined to handle formal scholarly analysis.

5.4   Incorporating Richer and More Complex Representations

Here, we have focused on reproducing text descriptions with frames and with general knowledge about the entities described. However, merely modeling natural language statements is likely to be incomplete unless the text is unusually comprehensive. For example, much of the information in newspapers is not in the text of articles but in tables, pictures, and advertisements. To capture this information and to incorporate sources such as diaries, letters, and other types of records, we may need to augment the text representations with non-linguistic frames or other types of knowledge structures. A wide range of models which incorporate increasing levels of external knowledge are possible. Among those are architectural description logics, shopping models, and models of relevant norms and legal concepts. It would also be helpful to expand beyond communities and coordinate our models with some of the GIS-based approaches from area studies and "smart cities" projects from urban planning and eventually community models could be merged and extended to become national or international models. Eventually, standards bodies could determine preferred approaches. We need to develop a representation environment that allows representations to be manipulated and used at different resolutions for different applications.

5.5   Interacting with the Structured Models

Structured complex representations should support novel types of user interaction. For instance, [2] described how multiple trails of causally related events could be presented through an interactive timeline. The model-oriented approach many also support question answering. Moreover, we might generate narratives and other types of discourse from the EntityLogs and EventLogs. More ambitiously, we might also develop interactive historical environments. We might teach students about the French Revolution by allowing them to explore simulations of communities involved in the French Revolution.

User interfaces are also needed to help authors create a structured corpus. We envision a workbench for historians to organize evidence and pursue hypotheses in their research. Indeed, the structure provided by the models can facilitate the evaluation of evidence and inferences and should highlight gaps and inconsistencies.

5.6   Incorporating Knowledge of Cultures and Broad Social Theories

The models developed here are intended to apply equally across cultures though we have focused on the US Midwest because its communities are especially well documented in historical newspapers. Even in the short passage about Minneapolis described above, we considered the social organization of the Dakotas. Specific conceptual frameworks could be developed bottom up, but cultural and social modeling may also be implemented top-down (e.g., [11]). Moreover, while these theories can be applied to help modeling, eventually the large amount of data being modeled may in turn be useful for evaluating the theories.

5.7   Alternative Architectures

While Java was effective for implementing behavior-based frames, several of the issues we have encountered are due to Java's design. Among these issues is ambiguity about the distinction between classes and instances; there is a need for several inheritance paths depending on context and for readily extensible representation of classes. As we discuss in [7], future modeling efforts should explore other object-oriented languages such as Self and Slate [13].

While our frame-based approach remains faithful to the text of historical sources in a way that is important for historians, for other applications some liberties may be allowed. Much in the way that historical fiction takes liberties with historical evidence, simulations may fill in gaps and provide engaging interaction with the users. Indeed, some historians would say that the point of studying history is finding insights into plausible underlying processes. Simulations might help with that. Simulations could also be implemented as multi-agent interactions. Further, we believe that simulations could be the basis of history-oriented games.

6   Conclusion

We have proposed that frame-based object-oriented modeling is useful as an approach to historical descriptions of communities. We explore issues and implications of this proposal by modeling a community which is comparable to many communities described in digitized historical documents. Specifically, we have explored models with frames which track English natural language statements and extended them with conceptual and real world knowledge. We focused on natural language because such models may help with indexing and access to the historical records. However, a range of other related models is possible. We could develop models of social interactions not based on natural language.

While there is understandable caution in dealing with situations as complex as community models, there would be considerable value in having an overarching framework. Indeed, a focus on a broad "architecture of cognition" has led to considerable progress in understanding cognition and a similar broad impact may be expected for modeling communities.

Many challenges remain, but we believe there is a great value in highly structured representation of histories for interaction with that content. By and large, these are not algorithmic problems; rather, they are problems of representation, robustness, and scale. We urge a coordinated initiative of digital historians, social scientists, and information scientists to develop and apply broad conceptual models. We believe that these substantial challenges would yield to a concerted effort.

References

1. Allen, R.B.: Improving Access to Digitized Historical Newspapers with Text Mining, Coordinated Models, and Formative User Interface Design. In: IFLA International Newspaper Conference: Digital Preservation and Access to News and Views, New Delhi, pp. 54–59 (2010), http://boballen.info/RBA/PAPERS/IFLA2010/IFLA2010proceedings.pdf
2. Allen, R.B.: Visualization, Causation, and History. In: iConference (2011), http://dx.doi.org/10.1145/1940761.1940835
3. Allen, R.B.: Developing a Knowledge-base to Improve Interaction with Collections of Historical Newspapers. In: IFLA WLIC, San Juan, PR (2011), http://conference.ifla.org/sites/default/files/files/papers/ifla77/188-allen-en.pdf
4. Allen, R.B.: Model-Oriented Information Organization: Part 1, The Entity-Event Fabric. D-Lib Magazine (2013), doi:10.1045/july2013-allen-pt1

5. Allen, R.B.: Model-Oriented Information Organization: Part 2, Discourse Relationships. D-Lib Magazine (July 2013), doi:10.1045/july2013-allen-pt2
6. Allen, R.B.: Toward an Interactive Directory for Norfolk, Nebraska: 1899-1900. In: IFLA Newspaper and Genealogy Section Meeting, Singapore (2013), http://arxiv.org/abs/1308.5395
7. Allen, R.B.: Rich Semantic Modeling with Object-Oriented Approaches, ArXiv (in preparation)
8. Allen, R.B., Japzon, A., Achananuparp, P., Lee, K.-J.: A Framework for Text Processing and Supporting Access to Collections of Digitized Historical Newspapers. In: Smith, M.J., Salvendy, G. (eds.) HCII 2007. LNCS, vol. 4558, pp. 235–244. Springer, Heidelberg (2007)
9. Engeström, Y.: Innovative Learning in Work Teams: Analyzing Cycles of Knowledge Creation in Practice. In: Engestrom, Y., Miettinen, R., Punamaki, R. (eds.) Perspectives on Activity Theory: Learning in Doing: Social, Cognitive, and Computational Perspectives, pp. 377–404. Cambridge University Press, Cambridge (1999)
10. Fillmore, C.: Frame Semantics and the Nature of Language. Annals of the New York Academy of Sciences: Conference on the Origin and Development of Language and Speech 280, 20–32 (1976), http://www.icsi.berkeley.edu/pubs/ai/framesemantics76.pdf
11. Mohr, J.W., White, H.C.: How to Model an Institution. Theory and Society 37, 485–512 (2008), http://www.soc.ucsb.edu/ct/pages/JWM/Papers/How%20to%20Model%20an%20In./How%20to%20Model%20an%20Institution.pdf
12. Ruppenhofer, J., Ellsworth, M., Petruck, M.R.L., Johnson, C.R., Scheffczyk, J.: FrameNet II: Extended Theory and Practice (2010), https://framenet.icsi.berkeley.edu/fndrupal/the_book
13. Salzman, L., Aldrich, J.: Prototypes with Multiple Dispatch: An Expressive and Dynamic Object Model. In: Gao, X.-X. (ed.) ECOOP 2005. LNCS, vol. 3586, pp. 312–336. Springer, Heidelberg (2005)
14. Winston, M.E., Chaffin, R., Herrmann, D.: A Taxonomy of Part-Whole Relations. Cognitive Science 11, 417–444 (1987), doi:10.1207/s15516709cog1104_2

Documenting Social Unrest: Detecting Strikes in Historical Daily Newspapers

Kalliopi Zervanou, Marten Düring, Iris Hendrickx, and Antal van den Bosch

Center for Language Studies, Radboud University Nijmegen, The Netherlands
{K.Zervanou,M.Düring,I.Hendrickx,A.vandenBosch}@let.ru.nl

Abstract. The identification of relevant historical sources such as newspapers and letters and the extraction of information from them is an essential part of historical research. In this work, our aim is the detection of relevant primary sources with the goal to support researchers working on a specific historical event. We focus on the historical daily Dutch newspaper archive of the National Library of the Netherlands and strike events that happened in the Netherlands during the 1980s. Using a manually compiled database of strikes in the Netherlands, we first attempt to find reports on those strikes in historical daily newspapers by automatically associating database records to the daily press of the time covering the same strike. Then, we generalise our methodology to detect strike events in the press not currently covered by the strikes database, and support in this way the extension of secondary historical resources. Our methods are evaluated against the manually constructed database of strikes.

1 Introduction

The increasing amount of available digitised sources for historical research has been gradually transforming historical research methods. Historians are gaining control of new computational methods that stem from research in language and information technologies. In historical research, facts and events reported in textual sources play an essential role in documenting history. Primary sources of historical information (such as letters and newspaper articles) and secondary historical sources (the products of historical research, such as biographies and research publications) constitute the principal research material of historical research. Currently, while such sources may be available in digital form, they are typically not easy to access. Historians face the problem of finding those sources and of identifying the material relevant to their research in pools of information scattered across various archives, libraries and collections, often lacking metadata annotations relevant to historians and the means to associate all relevant sources relating to a given historical event. In this work, we attempt to address this issue by first investigating a method for linking and associating primary to secondary historical sources and, subsequently, attempting to detect primary sources related to a given event automatically. For our case study, we focus on a

A. Nadamoto et al. (Eds.): SocInfo 2013 Workshops, LNCS 8359, pp. 120–133, 2014.
© Springer-Verlag Berlin Heidelberg 2014

specific type of events related to social unrest, strike events. Moreover, we focus on a specific period, the 1980s, and a specific country, the Netherlands.

Strikes, being indicators of social unrest, are events of particular interest for social historians. Unfortunately, long-term data collections on events related to labour unrest, such as strikes, exist for very few countries [12]. Much of the current databases are manually compiled by historians, primarily based on investigation of newspaper articles [12,18]. The development of language and information technology applications for this task may support computational historians by partly automating and speeding up the primary source analysis process. The period of the 1980s has been characterised by social unrest mainly due to a global economic recession in the developed countries that followed the 1973 oil crisis. It has been marked by the neoliberal financial policies of the Reagan administration in the US, which strived for a free market economy and tax cuts to stimulate economic growth [9], and thatcherism in the UK, where a policy of inflation control, privatisation of state industries and increasing restraints on trade unionism was accompanied by a surge of unemployment and numerous labour actions, the most notable being the 1984–85 Miners' Strike [7]. In the Netherlands, the economic depression of the 1980s is associated with wage cuts and increased unemployment. Many industries closed down or transferred their activities to countries offering cheap labour. The decrease of the number of industrial workers was accompanied by an increase of service sector employees who took the lead in labour action [18]. It was a period of *defensive strikes* against government measures [18], such as the strike against changes in the law on incapacity for work[1] [11] and strikes against unemployment and wage cuts, which culminated in the 1982 Wassenaar Agreement on wage regulation and part-time employment [18,10].

In our case study, we use an existing secondary source, a database of labour actions in the Netherlands [18] and the Digitised Daily Newspapers online collection of the National Library of the Netherlands, as a potentially rich source of primary historical information about strikes in the Netherlands reported in the daily press of the 1980s. In this paper, we start by a description of our historical sources in Section 2, followed in Section 3 by a description of our methodologies for associating primary to secondary sources and automatically detecting strike articles. In Section 4, we discuss our evaluation and results. We conclude in Section 5 with our remarks and observations related to this work and our plans for future work.

2 Historical Resources

The historical resources used in this study are of two types. The first is the database of labour actions in the Netherlands [18], which is a secondary historical source, the result of ongoing research on compiling all information related to Dutch labour actions. The second is a collection of primary sources, an online

---

[1] Wet op de Arbeidsongeschiktheid.

collection of historical Dutch newspapers, provided by the National Library of the Netherlands. In this section, we describe these sources in greater detail.

2.1   The Database of Labour Actions

The database of labour actions in the Netherlands is a historical resource created by the historian Dr van der Velden [18] for research purposes. It is an ongoing work, dedicated to the compilation of information on various types of labour actions in the Netherlands, dating as far back as 1372 and up to 2008[2] [17]. In this work, we only consider strike actions. A *strike* is defined as a specific type of labour action conforming to the following three criteria [19]:

  i. it is undertaken by employees only; student and farmer actions are not considered;
 ii. it involves a temporary interruption of work;
iii. it is a collective action, involving the participation of at least two persons.

The database has a relational structure, consisting of 32 linked tables. The most important attribute fields for each record are illustrated in Fig. 1, which depicts a screenshot of the online search interface[3].

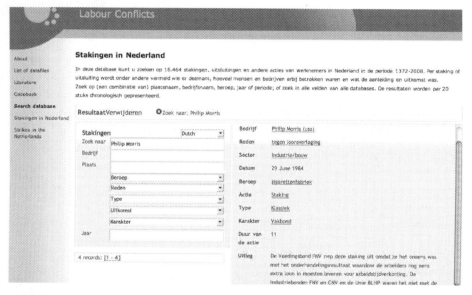

Fig. 1. Database of labour actions in the Netherlands online search interface

The database contains information about the type of labour action (e.g., strike, lock-out, demonstration), the dates, duration, companies affected, industrial sectors, number of participants, type of participants (e.g. women, young

---

[2] Data on strikes prior to 1810 is fragmentary. Our version of the data is from September 2012.

[3] http://socialhistory.org/en/stakingen

workers, immigrants), trade unions and chambers of commerce involved, reasons, locations, outcomes and information sources. We should note that all fields do not always contain full information about the respective action. For example, there are cases where the exact date is unknown and the database record states only the month or the year. Moreover, information about the action's exact location or profession might be too general (e.g. nation-wide, general), or even unknown. There is also a text field *Report (Verslag/Uitleg)*, containing notes in free-text form, mainly copied from the original sources of the information, along with some other notes of the historian. The information on the historical resources used (i.e. *Source (Bron)*) refers to a variety of sources, such as trade union meeting minutes, books, or newspapers articles. Once these sources become available in digitised form, the methods proposed in this work could be used to associate the database information to their original source.

2.2   The Historical Dutch Newspaper Collection

The historical Dutch newspaper collection[4] is an online collection of digitised daily newspapers dating from 1618 to 1995 [6]. It is the result of a digitisation project, the *Databank of Daily Digital Newspapers*[5] which has been initiated in 2006 by the National Library of the Netherlands aiming at digitising and providing online access to eight million pages of daily Dutch newspapers. An 8% of the 8,000 available newspaper titles have been selected for digitisation, based on a variety of importance criteria. The digitised data is in XML format, following Dublin Core [4] metadata standards. The newspapers have undergone OCR processing, and the various newspaper sections have been semi-automatically segmented. The metadata provided include newspaper title, page, section type (e.g., article, advertisement), publication and digitisation dates, author, and publisher. We should mention here that the KB newspaper collection often contains different OCR versions of the same article.

The digitised newspapers are accessible online at the National Library website[6], where a search interface is provided. Moreover, the archive is also accessible via a *Search/Retrieval via URL* (SRU) interface [14]. The data accessible via the National Library online interface include all metadata, text and article image, whereas via the SRU, the user may have access to metadata and text only. In this work, we use the SRU interface to send our automated queries to the collection. SRU is a standard XML-based search protocol for internet search queries which exploits the HTTP GET method for message transfer [8]. The queries are formed in CQL (Contextual Query Language), a query language designed not only to be intuitive and human readable, but also more powerful than boolean search (Google-type) engine languages [8]. The SRU search interface allows for keyword-based search in newspaper segments classified as articles in the collection and published at a specific date, or date range. It supports regular expression

---

[4] Historische Kranten: `http://kranten.kb.nl/`
[5] Databank Digitale Dagbladen.
[6] `http://kranten.kb.nl/`

patterns, where for example, the pattern `stak?n*` may match in the article, various words, such as *staking, staken, stakingacties, stakingen*. Finally, it allows for logical operators, such as `TermA AND TermB`, or `TermA OR TermB`. An example of a basic SRU query is illustrated in Fig. 2.

```
http://jsru.kb.nl/sru/sru?version=1.2&maximumRecords=1&
operation=searchRetrieve&startRecord=1&
recordSchema=ddd&
x-collection=DDD_artikel&
query=(dc.type=artikel
and date within "07-01-1980 13-01-1980"
and stak?n*)
```

Fig. 2. Sample SRU query URL for any article published in the second week of January 1980 containing the term pattern *stak?n**

While this form of querying is quite powerful, it poses also certain constraints on the complexity of the query made. In particular, it is difficult to constrain and refine the results, based e.g., on a number of optionally matched terms. Moreover, the SRU interface poses limitations on the number of terms one may use, since URLs have character length limitations. Thus, it is difficult to pose a general query, containing e.g., 100 terms. Finally, SRU by definition constrains the search to a keyword-based search. It does not allow for more refined querying, such as one that would include term weighting, or one that would be sensitive to domain-specific semantic categories such as "profession" or "trade union", as the latter are not included in the collection general metadata.

3   Detecting Strikes in Historical Daily Newspapers

Our approach in detecting strike events in historical newspaper articles has two objectives. The first is the association of existing records in the strikes database to respective information about these strikes in the press. The second objective is to propose a general method for retrieving articles related to strike events, so as to eventually support historians in their research, by providing the means to retrieve information about a given historical event of interest. In this section, we start in Section 3.1, by a description of the methodology for associating of database strike records to respective articles. Then, we describe in Section 3.2, how this data is used for generalising our method in retrieving strike articles, without any specific database record information.

3.1   Finding Information about Recorded Strikes in the Daily Press

For the purposes of our case study, we have selected a set of 60 database records from all strikes in the 1980s. The selection of the records was based on information about the strike duration, set to 1-20 days, and the minimum number of participants in the strike, set to 200 strikers. This filtering of database records aimed at the selection of fairly important strikes which are more likely to be reported in the newspapers collection of the National Library of the Netherlands.

We then use the database record values referring to *strike date, strikers profession, location, province, chamber of commerce, and trade unions* involved, as query terms for our automated SRU queries to the collection. If any of these values is missing from the database, the respective field is ignored and the query is formed with the remaining values. In transforming the database record field values into query terms we explicitly ignore terms such as *algemeen* (general), *arbeiders* (workers), *personeel* (personnel), *landelijk* (nation-wide) which are too general for performing a query, since they do not specify a particular location or profession. The date range used in the query spans from a week before to a week after the strike date mentioned in the database. Finally, the term pattern `stak?n*` was always added to the database record terms. This process resulted in retrieving 3,300 articles, which are subsequently filtered based on the number of database field categories that are matched in the text. 685 articles were found matching at least 2 categories. Out of these, we have manually annotated 424. We have stopped the annotation process at that stage, because we considered that we had enough annotated data for the article training sample that we needed. The objective of the manual metadata annotation was to find articles referring to strikes, or strike threats, and classify them according to the categories illustrated in Table 1. This annotated set of articles is subsequently used as a training sample in acquiring more general terms, independently from specific database records, as discussed in the following section, Section 3.2.

Table 1. Manual annotation categories of articles

Annotation	Description
SF	The article refers to the strike (S) in question and is fully (F) dedicated to it.
SFb	The article fully refers to a strike but not the one in question.
SP	The article partially (P) refers to the strike (S) in question.
TF	This article is fully (F) dedicated to a strike threat (T) of the strike in question.
TFb	This article fully refers to a strike threat, but not the one in question.
TP	This article is partially (P) dedicated to a strike threat (T) of the strike in question.
ERROR	This article is not about a strike or a strike threat.

3.2   Retrieving Articles Referring to Strike Actions

In order to generalise our method, so as to retrieve articles related to strikes without reference to a specific database strike record, we extract a set of strong keywords from our data that could be used independently of the database.

We extract these keywords from the set of articles found to refer to a strike and a set of random articles. The objective in this phase is to identify those keywords which best describe strike articles and distinguish such articles from the rest. For this purpose, we start by linguistically processing both sets of strike and random articles, using natural language processing tools. Then, we apply statistical measures on the content words of the articles to identify distinguishing keyword terms. In this section, we describe in more detail the tools and the methods used for these tasks.

Natural Language Processing. For linguistic processing, we apply in our method the *Frog* suite of natural language tools for Dutch [15]. This suite of software tools analyses text documents, so as to identify in text grammatical and semantic information. For this kind of analysis, the *Frog* tools rely on TiMBL[3], a memory-based classifier engine for automatically learning the linguistic categories required, based on examples of annotated text. *Frog* initially applies tokenisation and lemmatisation on the articles, i.e. it splits the text into words and identifies the morphological characteristics of these words, such as affixes and compounds. Then, it applies part-of-speech and named entity recognition, so as to grammatically classify a given word as a noun, an adjective, etc., and assign semantic categories to proper nouns, such as locations, persons and organisations.

The output of *Frog* is used to select content words found in our articles, i.e. nouns, verbs, participles and adjectives, and to filter away proper nouns (i.e. names of people, organizations, locations, etc.). Linguistic filtering is an approach that is commonly used in term and keyword extraction (e.g., [2,5,20,1]). The rationale behind our type of word filtering is based on the hypothesis that content words are the indicators of the informational content in a document. Moreover, proper nouns, although they are highly informational about a given strike event, are too specific for an application of a general keyword-based query for strike articles.

Statistical Measures. For the selection of keywords that best distinguish strike articles among other articles, we combine two statistical measures: $tf \cdot idf$ score and χ^2.

Term frequency - inverse document frequency, $(tf \cdot idf)$ [1], is a measure commonly used in information retrieval applications which is used to measure how different the frequency of a given term is in a particular document when compared to its frequency in the whole document collection. It is calculated as the product of the term frequency in a given document by the inverse frequency of this term in the entire collection (i.e. how rare the term is in the collection). In our approach, we calculate the frequency of the selected content words in an article and take the product of this frequency by the inverse frequency of the given word in a document collection of 366,000 Dutch newspaper articles from the late 1990s.

Next, the χ^2 *measure* is applied to the $tf \cdot idf$ score to determine to which extent a given word's $tf \cdot idf$ score varies from the mean, thus distinguishing terms that are more characteristic for strike articles compared to others. We computed the χ^2 values on a dataset of 692 news articles that contained 50% strike related articles and 50% random articles. The results of the χ^2 statistical scoring are sorted based on χ^2 score; the top 50 keywords are selected as being the most characteristic for strike articles. Fig. 3 illustrates those keywords in Dutch and their respective English translations. A quick observation that one can make is that variants of the word *strike* are quite prominent. Moreover, we notice words, such as *trade unions, workers, union, company, conflict, negotiations* which are also quite characteristic of articles referring to strikes. Most notably, we observe words such as *CBA* (collective labour agreement), *fired, working hours reduction*, and *government* which also point to core issues related to strikes in the Netherlands during the 1980s: strikes against government measures, against unemployment, and the issues related to working hours reduction.

---

staking, directie, acties, werknemers, stakers, bond, stakingen, werk, bonden, bedrijf, personeel, woordvoerder, actie, gestaakt, staken, redactie, vakbonden, produktie, werkweek, akkoord, gaan, mensen, stakingsacties, gegaan, overleg, onderhandelingen, 36-urige, uur, arbeidstijdverkorting, stil, wil, werkgevers, bedrijven, werkwilligen, week, plat, poort, fabriek, onbepaalde, conflict, besloten, eisen, cao, invoering, gedwongen, leden, regering, stakende, rechter, ontslagen

---

strike, management, actions, workers, strikers, union, strikes, work, unions, business, staff, spokesman, action, struck, striking, editorial, trade unions, production, work week, agreement, go, people, strike action, gone, deliberation, negotiations, 36-hour, hour, working hours reduction, still, will, employers, companies, willing to work, week, flat, port, factory, indefinite, conflict, decided, demands, cba, introduction, forced, members, government, striking, judge, fired

---

Fig. 3. Top-50 keywords found based on χ^2 weights and respective English translation

4   Evaluation and Results

In this section, we present the evaluation methodology we adopted for our two article retrieval methods:

i. **DB record method:** the method where we retrieve and link articles to specific database records, using as query terms the respective record fields;
ii. χ^2 **term method:** the method where we attempt to discover strike articles independently of specific database records.

For the evaluation of our methods, we consider that the strikes mentioned in the database constitute a complete recording of all strike events in the 1980s. We thus compare the articles retrieved by our methods to this golden standard in terms of Pearson's correlation coefficient [13]. We opt at this stage of our experiments for computing correlation, because it can give us a comparative indication for the entire dataset period of the 1980s of how well our methods perform compared to the actual database strike records. The more precise and more typical evaluation metrics of precision and recall, commonly used for evaluating retrieval tasks but requiring manual annotation of article relevance, can be estimated at a later stage for those data periods where we identify discrepancies between the database records and the articles retrieved, so as to get a more detailed picture of the results. In our evaluation, we compare our *DB record method* and χ^2 *term method* to two baseline methods:

i. **stak?n* baseline:** a method that retrieves articles merely based on the term pattern stak?n*;
ii. **DB NE terms baseline:** a method that uses lists of named entities, such as profession, trade union, location, etc. from the database.

The first method is the baseline that shows what can be retrieved of strike related articles by simply looking for the variants of the word 'strike', emulating a simple Google-like keyword search. The second baseline method, the DB NE method uses some knowledge from the strikes database. In particular, the DB NE method uses knowledge about named entities in the database to form general strike action queries. Since it is using database knowledge, it is expected to score relatively well in correlating with the occurrence of strikes according to the database. However, the DB NE method would be difficult to apply for historical events, where a full knowledge base of possible actors and locations is unknown. All methods, including our proposed DB record and χ^2 term methods, are used to query the newspaper collection for articles, for every week of the 1980s period, for 522 weeks in total. All methods include the (baseline) term pattern stak?n* in the query.

In order to assess all methods, we first use the stak?n* baseline method, to retrieve articles using a fairly simple query (such as the one illustrated in Fig.2). Subsequently, for assessing the performance of the other methods, we filter our results based on the respective method query terms. For our DB record method, these terms are acquired by the strike database records corresponding to a given week. For our χ^2 term method, these terms are the set of the top 50 χ^2 terms, and for the DB NE baseline method, these terms are the 11,430 single- and multiword phrases denoting entities, such as professions, trade unions and locations. We perform this query term filtering to overcome the limitations posed by the SRU query, namely the limitations on query length and the limitations on refining our queries based on semantic categories specific to our domain (for the DB record and the DB NE terms methods) and on assigning term weighting (such as χ^2 weights). Finally, we use the training set of manually annotated articles to define keyword and category matching scores and thresholds for each method applied, which would optimally separate strike articles from other articles.

For our χ^2 method, the article ranking score is a score that combines χ^2 weights for the terms matched in the article, normalised by the article length in tokens (words). It is calculated as follows:

$$score = \frac{\Sigma\chi^2}{L} \qquad (1)$$

where $\Sigma\chi^2$ denotes the sum of χ^2 weights for the terms matched in the article and L is the document length in tokens. After our experiments with the training articles, the optimal threshold T for this score is set to 3.59.

For the DB NE terms baseline method, the ranking score combines the number of named entity term categories matched in the article with the total number of matches found for the term pattern stak?n* normalised by the article length in tokens:

$$score = C + \frac{S}{L} \qquad (2)$$

where C is the total number of database named entity term categories matched in the article, S is the frequency of stak?n* pattern matches, and L is the document length in tokens. For this method, our experiments show that the optimal threshold T is 3.032.

Finally, as also discussed in Section 3.1 above, for the DB records method, we select the articles matching at least two categories of the database record fields.

Figure 4 graphically illustrates the results of all methods. As seen in Figure 4, strike articles represent a small percentage, mostly below 2%, of the total articles published in this period. The stak?n* baseline method results, indicated in pink, have a higher recall of articles, whereas our χ^2 keywords method and the DB NE terms method, in purple and green colour respectively, have more precise results. An interesting point is that those methods often exhibit peaks in periods where there are not any strikes reported in the database records (the latter indicated in black colour), such as for example in January 1984, where manual inspection of the results indicates that articles mainly report about a big strike of bauxite miners in Surinam (the former Dutch colony which had become independent from the Netherlands in 1975) and the intervention of the army. Moreover, in March 1980, there seems to be a disproportionate media coverage of strikes, as illustrated by the DB record method results, indicated in yellow colour. We observe that while the DB record method results follow closely in general the actual strike records in the DB, in that particular period of March 1980, the DB record method retrieves more articles than in any other period. Manual inspection of the results indicates that there is ongoing unrest in various sectors, such as public transport, the Rotterdam port and the dairy industry, with strike threats and ongoing negotiations. As reported in these articles, the reason for this unrest all over Netherlands was the so-called *loonmaatregel*, namely a law that gives the power to the government to specify wages, rather than the agreed wages between workers unions and employers. This particular law is being discussed since December 1979 and in March 1980 the government is about to set it in effect. The various actions in various professional sectors that are taken in March

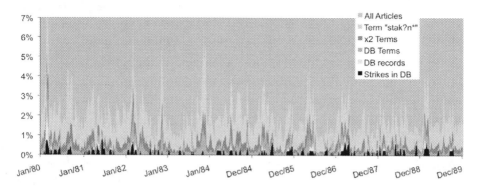

Fig. 4. Results: strike articles retrieved vs. all articles

Table 2. Retrieved strike articles correlation to strikes reported in the DB (per week)

Method	Correlation
$stak?n^*$ term	0.22
DB NE terms (T: 3.032)	0.36
χ^2 terms (T: 3.59)	0.30
DB record terms (T:2)	0.50

and the strike threats that are reported in the newspapers reflect the workers unions stance against this governmental intervention.

In Table 2, we can see in more detail the correlation of each method compared to the strikes reported in the database. Correlation is estimated in terms of Pearson's correlation coefficient [13] between the number of retrieved articles versus the number of actual strikes in the database, for every week in the 1980s, i.e. 522 data points for every method under consideration.

The lowest correlation is displayed by the `stak?n*` baseline method, which achieves a mere 0.22. Interestingly, the best result that one may achieve is 0.50, by the DB record method, with a threshold of 2 or more matched categories and with a query of a week range that matches exactly the database week date. Our χ^2 keywords method, which has no specific knowledge about database records and searches with a set of topical keywords, performs only slightly below the DB NE terms method. Both perform better than the `stak?n*` baseline, but worse than the DB record method. We have to note at this point that, as also mentioned in Section 2.1, the information in the database records is neither always complete, nor always specific. Thus, there are cases where the record fields do not mention an exact location, or a specific profession, or workers union etc., because it is either unknown or too general (e.g. workers, nation-wide). In such cases, the respective fields are ignored in the query formation. So, we may have cases where a record can not really provide enough information to form a query for the newspaper collection, or provide a query where only one category will be known and the resulting articles would not pass our "at least 2 categories" threshold. This issue of underspecified information in the database records entails that the DB record method can never really reach correlation 1 with the database. Moreover, the newspaper collection often contains articles that are different OCR versions of the same article. This often results in having a big number of articles retrieved that in essence are the same story. This issue of duplication also affects our correlation results, while not directly affecting the actual results quality. Manual assessment in terms of precision and recall will provide a better insight in the results.

5   Conclusion

In this work, we have presented and compared a method for associating and linking primary to secondary historical sources. We have used strike labour actions in the Netherlands in the 1980s as a case study, and have attempted to link two available resources: a database of labour actions in the Netherlands and a digitised collection of historical daily Dutch newspapers. We compared two methods: one in which database records were encoded as queries, and query-based searches were performed directly on the newspaper archive per database record, and one which used a single complex query composed of strike-related terms that was applied to the entire time range of our case study.

Articles referring to strikes constitute a small percentage of the articles published in the press; although they can peak at 7% of all articles, they mostly constitute a proportion below 2%. Finding relevant articles thus requires a fair amount of precision. Our initial experiments in linking database strike records to respective news articles in the press achieve encouraging results. Our single-query method, using χ^2-based selection of 50 terms most specifically related to strikes, performs almost comparably to a method using a set of 11,430 single- and multiword keywords from the entities denoting trade unions, companies, professions and location names in the database.

Our experiments in retrieving strike articles also reveal the inherent limitations of the keyword-based method: values around 0.3 indicate a low correlation. The method that generates queries from individual database records achieves a substantially higher correlation of 0.50 — which is still only moderate. This moderate correlation highlights two underlying issues in our data, the underspecification of information in the database and the duplication issue in the newspaper collection. Since the database records do not always specify enough information to form a query, because the information is either unknown or too general, the DB record method can never really reach correlation 1 with the database. Moreover, since the newspaper collection contains multiple OCR versions of the same article, the number of articles retrieved can often be disproportionate in terms of correlation to the strikes in the database, while the actual information retrieved is not erroneous. Manual evaluation in terms of precision and recall is expected to provide more refined evaluation results.

Still our analysis on global correlation for the entire period of the 1980s highlighted periods of interest for manual observation. It showed that low correlations can have hidden causes that may be interesting to historical research, if only as a serendipitous side-effect. We found an insubordinate number of news articles in January 1984 describing miner strikes in Surinam, a former colony which was still closely monitored in the 1980s in the Netherlands. Likewise, we found a large amount of strike-related news in March 1984 which was related more to strike threats and negotiations, indicating a period of discontent with the governmental policy on wages. In previous work, we developed a prototype method for learning to classify news articles reporting on strike threats rather than strikes [16], which could be integrated with the current work.

As other future work we plan to experiment with a combination of χ^2 keywords and database entity terms, and expand our evaluation with standard metrics from information retrieval (precision, recall, F-score, average precision). Most importantly, we shall attempt to use document classification methods instead of filtering, so as to refine our retrieval. Finally, the next step will be the investigation of the evolution in time of a given strike event, with detection of all associated sub-events, such as strike threats, negotiations, announcements and court interventions.

Acknowledgments. This work has been carried out within the framework of the Digging into Data project ISHER[7], which aims at analysing and associating social history text documents, so as to improve access and support historical research. The authors wish to thank Sjaak van der Velden for his support with the Database of Labour Actions in the Netherlands; Marian Hellema, Anouk Janssen, and Rene Voorburg from the National Library of the Netherlands for their support in accessing the Dutch Daily Newspaper collection.

References

1. Baeza-Yates, R., Ribeiro-Neto, B.: Modern Information Retrieval. Addison Wesley Longman (1999)
2. Bourigault, D., Gonzalez-Mullier, I., Gros, C.: LEXTER, a Natural Language Tool for Terminology Extraction. In: 7th EURALEX Intl. Congress on Lexicography, Part II, pp. 771–779. Göteborg University, Göteborg (1996)
3. Daelemans, W., Van den Bosch, A.: Memory-based language processing. Cambridge University Press, Cambridge (2005)
4. DCMI: Dublin Core Metadata Initiative, http://dublincore.org/
5. Jacquemin, C.: Spotting and Discovering Terms through Natural Language Processing. MIT Press, Cambridge (2001)
6. Klijn, E.: Databank of digital daily newspapers: moving from theory to practice. News from the IFLA Section on Newspapers (19), 8–9 (2009)
7. Lyddon, D.: The 1984–85 miners' strike. In: TUC History Online. London Metropolitan University and the Trades Union Congress (2013), http://www.unionhistory.info/timeline/1960_2000_Narr_Display_2.php?Where=NarTitle+contains+%27The+1984-85+Miners+Strike%27+

[7] Integrated Social History Environment for Research – Digging into Social Unrest: http://www.diggingintodata.org/Home/AwardRecipientsRound22011/ISHER/tabid/ 196/Default.aspx

8. McCallum, S.: A look at new information retrieval protocols: SRU, OpenSearch/A9, CQL, and Xquery. In: The World Library and Information Congress: 72nd IFLA General Conference and Council, Seoul, Korea (2006)
9. Niskanen, W.A.: Reaganomics. In: Henderson, D.R. (ed.) Concise Encyclopedia of Economics, 1st edn. Library of Economics and Liberty (1992), http://www.econlib.org/library/Enc1/Reaganomics.html
10. Parlementair Documentatie Centrum: Parlement & politiek, Universiteit Leiden, http://www.parlement.com/id/vh8lnhrqszxy/akkoord_van_wassenaar_1982
11. Rommelse, A.F.: Een geschiedenis van het arbeidsongeschiktheidsbeleid in Nederland. Research memorandum, Department of Economics, Universiteit Leiden (February 2011)
12. Silver, B.: Forces of Labor. Workers' Movements and Globalization since 1870. Cambridge University Press, New York (2003)
13. Stigler, S.M.: Francis galton's account of the invention of correlation. Statistical Science 4(2), 73–79 (1989)
14. The Library of Congress: SRU – Search/Retrieval via URL, http://www.loc.gov/standards/sru/
15. Van den Bosch, A., Busser, G., Daelemans, W., Canisius, S.: An efficient memory-based morphosyntactic tagger and parser for dutch. In: van Eynde, F., Dirix, P., Schuurman, I., Vandeghinste, V. (eds.) Selected Papers of the 17th Computational Linguistics in the Netherlands Meeting, Leuven, Belgium, pp. 99–114 (2007)
16. Van den Hoven, M., Van den Bosch, A., Zervanou, K.: Beyond reported history: Strikes that never happened. In: Darányi, S., Lendvai, P. (eds.) Proceedings of the First International AMICUS Workshop on Automated Motif Discovery in Cultural Heritage and Scientific Communication Texts, Vienna, Austria, pp. 20–28 (2010)
17. Van der Velden, S.: Database of dutch labour actions, https://collab.iisg.nl/web/labourconflicts/datafiles
18. Van der Velden, S.: Stakingen in Nederland. Arbeidersstrijd 1830–1995. Stichting Beheer IISG/NIWI, Amsterdam, The Netherlands (2000)
19. Van der Velden, S.: Werknemers in actie. Twee eeuwen stakingen, bedrijfsbezettingen en andere acties in Nederland. Aksant, Amsterdam (2004)
20. Witten, I., Paynter, G., Frank, E., Gutwin, C., Nevill-Manning, C.: KEA: Practical Automatic Keyphrase Extraction. In: 4th ACM Conf. on Digital Libraries, Berkeley, CA, USA, pp. 254–255 (August 1999)

Collective Memory in Poland: A Reflection in Street Names*

Radoslaw Nielek[1], Aleksander Wawer[2], and Adam Wierzbicki[1]

[1] Polish-Japanese Institue of Information Technology,
ul. Koszykowa 86., 02-008 Warsaw, Poland
{nielek,adamw}@pjwstk.edu.pl
[2] Institue of Computer Science Polish Academy of Science,
ul. Jana Kazimierza 5, Warsaw, Poland
axw@ipipan.waw.pl

Abstract. Our article starts with an observation that street names fall into two general types: generic and historically inspired. We analyse street names distributions (of the second type) as a window to nation-level collective memory in Poland. The process of selecting street names is determined socially, as the selections reflect the symbols considered important to the nation-level society, but has strong historical motivations and determinants. In the article, we seek for these relationships in the available data sources. We use Wikipedia articles to match street names with their textual descriptions and assign them to the time points. We then apply selected text mining and statistical techniques to reach quantitative conclusions. We also present a case study: the geographical distribution of two particular street names in Poland to demonstrate the binding between history and political orientation of regions.

Keywords: collective memory, Wikipedia, street names.

1 Introduction

The idea behind this article is based on an observation that the choice of street names is a reflection of selective properties of national collective memory. The choice of street names reflects what is worth remembering and what is important, how we want to remember the past.

The notion of collective memory comes from a French sociologist Maurice Halbwachs [5]. He distinguishes three types of memory: autobiographical (personal, individual memory), collective (group memory that maintains society's interpretations of the past) and historical (shaped by historians).

Collective memory has been the subject of numerous scholarly publications in the fields of sociology, cultural anthropology and history, too numerous to list here. The attempts to investigate it using computational means are relatively new and few, mostly associated with text mining historical corpora.

* This work is supported by Polish National Science Centre grant 2012/05/B/ST6/03364.

A. Nadamoto et al. (Eds.): SocInfo 2013 Workshops, LNCS 8359, pp. 134–142, 2014.

The studies of street names distributions are exclusively the domain of computational cartography. For instance, [8] analyze patterns and relations underlying the selection of European cities as names of German streets. Their analysis is focused on spatial proximity and does not consider historical factors (as the authors explicitly put it: *factors like bilateral or historical relations of cities are relevant for selective cities and can be seen as noise*). Takahashi et al. [7] has tried to predict importance of historical events based link structure of Wikipedia entities. Application of NLP tools and text mining approach for studying historical documents has been quite well researched starting from five thousand years old Sumerian clay tablets[6] through 19th and 20th century books [3] and ending with computational history of the ACL [1]. Au Yeung et al. [2] have tried to study collective memory about historical events by extraction references to the past in news articles.

The paper is organized as follows: Section 2 describes the data sources used in the analyses, Section 3 describes historical mappings of streets names. Section 4 describes the result of machine learning and text mining experiments on Wikipedia articles. Section 5 is the case study of geographical distribution of two historically-linked street names. We conclude in Section 6.

2   Dataset

Dataset with names of all streets in Poland has been obtained from the TERYT[1] as a XML file. Every street is accompanied with three numbers that identify province, district and community. Number of all streets exceeds 247 thousands but only ca. 35 thousands names are unique (the most popular street name is Polna[2] and occurs 3132 times). Words like street, square, boulevard etc. have been removed from the dataset because of two reasons. First, differences between street, alley or square are not important for our research goal (we do not want to treat separately same street patrons because in some cities their name is given to street and in other to square). Second, street/square/boulevard prefix is useless for matching street names with Wikipedia entities. All street names composed of less than two words were removed to clear the dataset from ordinary words like Green Street or Long Street (and leaving only historical events and names; in Polish, combinations of name and surname are used to identify people, streets and all historical events are also named with the use of at least two words). After the data clearance the dataset contained 16635 street names matched with entries in the Polish Wikipedia.

The process of matching Wikipedia entries with streets names faced many surprising difficulties. First of all, street names in Polish are in other casing than the titles of entries in Wikipedia. Therefore, an automatic conjunction of all street names was needed (it is not a trivial task in Polish as many nouns and names are irregular and many people's names have foregin roots). The dataset

---

[1] TERYT is a National Official Register of the Territorial Division of the Country and is used by Polish administration for many location-related services.

[2] The adjective polna can be translated as field or wild.

contains also some misspellings but even bigger issue was an omissions of second given names and quite random order of names and surnames. Therefore, we ignored word order. Yet another problem was caused by abbreviations in names and titles.

To address previously mentioned issue,s a special function that measure similarity between street name and entries has been designed. Streets have been connected with the most similar entity, but only if similarity measure exceeded certain threshold (selected experimentally). Additionally to automatic matching, all non-matched streets and 25% of matched streets (selected according to a frequency of occurrence) have been checked manually. The final dataset[3] contains 8060 street names with their corresponding entries in Wikipedia. For the remaining 8575 street names either no corresponding article on Polish Wikipedia existed or matching could not be done unambiguously.

The drawback of the approach presented in previous paragraphs is that results may be biased by an existence of entries on the Polish Wikipedia (some type of people or topics may be systematically omitted by Wikipedia editors). Wikipedia is known as high quality (but not error-free), extensive encyclopedia and the Polish version is one of the biggest over the world with over one million of articles. Additionally, as neither sentiment nor opinion are extracted and used in this research even biased, bad quality articles with a lot of omissions may be useful. On the other hand a manual check of the matching results has revealed that for some street names corresponding article does not exist. A closer look on biographies of these missing people may be extremely interesting task but has not been done as a part of this study.

3   Street Names and Historical Links

From each Wikipedia article associated with a street name we extracted a set of year-alike numbers using regular expressions. We sorted the list and computed its median value as the most representative for an article. The experiments demonstrate that the method is nearly error-free in matching street names to historical periods and selecting the most prominent dates.

Figure 1 presents street frequencies plotted against the time line of extracted median years.

Dates related to street names cannot be seen as an indicator of when particular street has been built. Names for streets are selected from the whole Polish history. The only rule is that people are honored with naming streets only after dead.

Generally, it appears that the number of street names related to dates before 1800 is very low. Each street name, mapped to the period before 1500, represents either a king or a queen. The period of 1500-1700 is marked by two writers (Rej and Kochanowski), one artist (Stwosz) and two kings. Interestingly, only successful, militarily victorious rulers appear on the list.

---

[3] The final dataset is publicly available and can be downloaded from:
   http://nielek.pl/histoinformatics2013/8060streetnames.csv

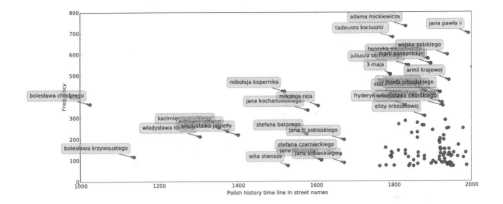

Fig. 1. Frequencies of street names mapped on historical time line. To improve readability only the most common name in given periods were labeled.

The period after 1800 is entirely different: there are many more associated street names and their structure is distinct. The period of 19th century is often considered as the time of national awakening, the raise of social programs to establish unique national identities, connected to language and rooted in local symbolic space (nation-language states). Therefore, it is hardly surprising that the most frequent street names (matched to the period after 1800) belong to the spiritual leaders such as romantic poets (Mickiewicz and Slowacki) and the pope (John Paul II of Polish origin), the most notable romantic composer (Chopin) and a novel writer (Sienkiewicz). All these figures and their works form a symbolic space (a canon) which defines Polish nationality and is a vehicle of national identity. It forms what might be considered a body of romantic nationalism, a developing imagined community of Poles with its spiritual value, unique character and language.

The timing of such ideas is not specific to Poland and shares many similarities with other countries. In fact, many nations were created using principles based on romantic nationalism as the source of legitimacy, emphasizing the binding between language and nation.

The period after 1800 overlaps with important changes in social and economic structure: industrialization. The intensification of nation-building efforts and rise of nationalism in this specific period are, according to Ernst Gellner [4], a side effect of industrial changes. In order to ensure availability of technically skilled work force, a state must enforce cultural standardisation, which is achieved by unification of political and the national (nationalism). The frequency of street names associated with nation-building leaders is therefore a consequence, or a reflection of pushing to unify the national and political, and as such fits in Gellner's conceptual framework.

4   Mining Street Name Frequencies

This section describes the result of machine learning and text mining experiments on the Wikipedia articles.

4.1   Predicting Street Name Frequencies

Number of street name occurrence may be seen as a rough estimation of importance of given person or event. As particular street name can appear only once in each city (there are some exception when one person appears under two names, e.g. Karol Wojtyla and pope John Paul II), many occurrences of the same street names in the dataset require that a lot of local communities decide to honor this particular person or event. The aim of the research presented in this section is to check whether the importance of people and historical events for society can be predicted based on features extracted from the Wikipedia.

In the experiment, we use 8060 unique street names with corresponding Wikipedia articles. We focus on predicting how many times does a street name occur knowing only article text and variables computed over the text. The problem may be seen as a regression and thus appropriate performance measurement metrics include R^2 and Mean Squared Error (MSE).

We computed following feature spaces:

- F1: counts of positive sentiment sentiment (npos) words, negative sentiment (nneg) words and total number of words (ntot);
- F2: number of extracted years (nyrs), aggregated negative (sneg) and positive (spos) word sentiment, finally total number of words (ntot);
- F3: lexemes (unigrams) as bag-of-words (disregarding word order) vectors, TF-IDF weighted, computed on word base forms obtained by the means of morphological analysis.
- F4: wikipedia categories for each article.

Table 1 presents the results obtained using three regression algorithms: ordinary least squares linear regression (Linear), Ridge Regression (Ridge) and Support Vector Regression (SVR) – with a radial basis kernel of degree 3. All results were computed as average values in 4-fold cross-validation.

Table 1. Numbers of words and annotated text fragments

Algorithm	Linear		Ridge		SVR	
Measure	R^2	MSE	R^2	MSE	R^2	MSE
F1: npos, nneg, ntot	0.0256	910.00	0.0288	910.41	0.0202	950.24
F2: nyrs, spos, sneg, ntot	0.0288	910.41	0.0288	910.41	0.0206	950.24
F3: all lexemes	n/a	n/a	0.1052	1000.48	0.0260	954.99
F4: wikipedia categories	0.001	933.19	0.001	933.19	0.0246	954.99

The results demonstrate that on dense feature sets (F1 and F2) simpler algorithms such as least squares linear regression or ridge regression perform better. The improvement is apparent in both MSE and R^2. The SVR algorithm outperforms two other regression types on sparse and large data of lexemes (F3). However, the results are very preliminary and need a lot of fine-tuning, perhaps backed by other data sources, to achieve satisfactory performance. The values of R^2 are generally low. On average, the predictions are mistaken by around 30 street name occurrences (MSE).

4.2   Predicting Street Names from Wikipedia Texts

In the second experiment, we focus on predicting whether a Wikipedia article has at least one associated street name (regardless of actual frequency, provided it is non-zero). We begin with the same set of 8060 Wikipedia articles with corresponding street names, but narrow it to a subset of 5698 biographies (we remove all articles that are not biographies). We also pick a random set of the same size of articles – biographies linked to history of Poland, but without a corresponding street name.

The question here is a similar one to that of the previous section: is textual information of Wikipedia articles sufficient to predict whether there is a street name linked to the article. This time, the problem may be seen as a classification and thus appropriate performance measurement metrics include precision and recall.

We use feature space of all lexemes, called F3 in the previous section, and a Logistic Regression classifier. We report the results as averages in 10-fold cross-validation in Table 2.

Table 2. Precision and recall of predicting street names from Wikipedia biographies

Measure	Precision	Recall
Result	0.841	0.875

As much as the results of regression on street name frequencies appear preliminary, the classification experiment reported in this section seems very promising, as the baseline of a balanced data set (as in this case) is at 0.5. Wikipedia articles carry relevant information and the models predict the existence of street names with good performance.

5   1st vs 3th May

1st May (also known as "May Day") is ancient spring festival in Northern Hemisphere but also the International Workers Day. May 1st was established in 1950 as a public holiday in Poland and used to be the most important public holiday in communist-era in Poland. The celebration usually took the form of huge streets parades (hundreds of thousands participants). Participation in such parades was often seen as a support for communist government. Although it is not officially celebrated any more, it is still a public holiday. Two days later in calendar there is another important day for Poland. 3th May 1791 "the first constitution of its type in Europe[4]" has been declared in Warsaw. From 1919 till 1951 (with a break during the Second World War when Poland was occupied by Germany and Russia) 3th May was a public holiday. Polish communist government after students unrests in 1946 has forbidden an official celebration of this holiday. In 1990, one year after the fall of communism in Poland, 3th May has regain its status as a public holiday.

Attitude toward these two holidays is sometimes seen as rough approximation of evaluation of communist-era in Poland. Street names that honor International Workers Day used to be very common in Polish cities between 1950 and 1989 (quite often it was one of main streets in cities). After the fall of communism, 1st May streets have started slowly to disappear and new street names honoring anti-communists activists (e.g. Marshal Jozef Pilsudzki) and ideas that were fight back by communists (e.g. declaration of 3th May constitution) are getting more popular.

The process of changing street names is quite slow because it has to overcome peoples habits and status quo dictate. Additionally, there are not many completely black or white people in Polish history and their evaluation vary strongly. Crucial factors in evaluating events in history are political views. In Poland, as in almost all countries[5], exist very stable geographical patterns of political support. Western provinces tend to support left wing parties and Southeastern provinces are more conservative. According to Polish law local councils decide about street names, so the geographical patterns of political support should be also visible in a ratio of communist to anti-communist names.

To verify the hypothesis stated in previous paragraph two street names have been selected 1st May (communist) and 3th May (anti-communist). The ratio of anti-communist vs. communist names for provinces varies really strong from 0.27 for Opolskie (southwestern part of Poland) to 2.58 and 3.9 for Podkarpackie and Maopolskie (southeastern) respectively. Spearman correlation between calculated ratio and support for left/right wings candidates in the second round of the last presidential election[6] is 0.504. On fig. 2 a characteristic spatial pattern is visible where western and southwestern provinces are more left-oriented than center and eastern provinces.

---

[4] The first modern constitution was declared in the USA. The well-known French constitution was declared three months after the Polish constitution.

[5] For example in the USA democrats never win in so called redneck states like Texas or Kentucky and in Germany CSU (right wing party) rules in Bayern over 50 years in row.

[6] The last presidential election in Poland took place in April 2010. In second round voters could choose between Jaroslaw Kaczynski (right-wing party) and Bronislaw Komorowski (central/left-wing party).

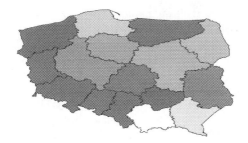

Fig. 2. Number of 3th May streets in comparison to 1st May streets in provinces. Darker color denotes lower value.

6   Conclusions

This paper describes computational experiments aimed at using a database of street names as a resource of investigating past, as reflected in collective memory of a nation.

The analyses described in this paper prove that street names are an important carrier of national identity and have strong historical connections. Using automated mapping of street names to their associated dates, we examine their distribution in time. We observe that the type of symbols, selected as street names, as well as their density, changes in time. The change overlaps with industrial revolution and may confirm Ernst Gellner's views on the birth of nationalism.

Dataset crafted for the research presented in the paper creates enormous opportunities for further studies. Connection of street names and demographic information about cities and communities may reveal interesting patterns. Exchanging an existing administrative division of Poland with it historical versions is another step worth considering. Furthermore, frequency of particular street names has been used as a rough estimation of street name importance but it may happened that some names are used very often but only for small streets on suburbs. Therefore, a metric that combines frequency and geospatial features (e.g. location, length) will be in future examined. Very interesting results can also be obtained by analyses whether selected street names are relating to local or national or global level. Using additional sources of historical information, next to Wikipedia, may improve coverage and add some missing features but will likely make an automatic analyses a nightmare.

References

1. Anderson, A., McFarland, D., Jurafsky, D.: Towards a computational history of the acl: 1980-2008. In: Proceedings of the ACL 2012 Special Workshop on Rediscovering 50 Years of Discoveries, ACL 2012, pp. 13–21. Association for Computational Linguistics, Stroudsburg (2012), http://dl.acm.org/citation.cfm?id=2390507.2390510

2. Au Yeung, C.M., Jatowt, A.: Studying how the past is remembered: towards computational history through large scale text mining. In: Proceedings of the 20th ACM International Conference on Information and Knowledge Management, CIKM 2011, pp. 1231–1240. ACM, New York (2011), http://doi.acm.org/10.1145/2063576.2063755
3. Gander, L., Lezuo, C., Unterweger, R.: Rule based document understanding of historical books using a hybrid fuzzy classification system. In: Proceedings of the 2011 Workshop on Historical Document Imaging and Processing, HIP 2011, pp. 91–97. ACM, New York (2011), http://doi.acm.org/10.1145/2037342.2037358
4. Gellner, E.: Nations and Nationalism. Cornell University Press (1983)
5. Halbwachs, M.: La Mémoire collective. Presses Universitaires de France (1950)
6. Jaworski, W.: Contents modelling of neo-sumerian ur iii economic text corpus. In: Proceedings of the 22nd International Conference on Computational Linguistics, COLING 2008, vol. 1, pp. 369–376. Association for Computational Linguistics, Stroudsburg (2008), http://dl.acm.org/citation.cfm?id=1599081.1599128
7. Takahashi, Y., Ohshima, H., Yamamoto, M., Iwasaki, H., Oyama, S., Tanaka, K.: Evaluating significance of historical entities based on tempo-spatial impacts analysis using wikipedia link structure. In: Proceedings of the 22nd ACM Conference on Hypertext and Hypermedia, HT 2011, pp. 83–92. ACM, New York (2011), http://doi.acm.org/10.1145/1995966.1995980
8. Thiel, S., Pippig, K., Burghardt, D.: Analysis of street names regarding the designation of cities. In: Buchroithner, M.F. (ed.) Proceedings of the 26th International Cartographic Conference. International Cartographic Association (2013)

Author Index